Department of Health and Social Security

Mental Handicap:
Progress, Problems and Priorities

A Review of Mental Handicap Services in England since the 1971 White Paper "Better Services for the Mentally Handicapped".

London: Her Majesty's Stationery Office

ISBN 0 11   321075 2

Foreword by Secretary of State for Social Services

This report on mental handicap policy was prepared by a team composed of officials from the Department of Health and Social Security and Professor Peter Mittler (formerly Chairman of the National Development Group for the Mentally Handicapped) with observers from other departments concerned. The team was set up by my predecessor to provide a comprehensive survey of progress made since the 1971 White Paper "Better Services for the Mentally Handicapped", and was continued with my full approval. I saw it as essential to assess the progress made towards the White Paper targets for 1991, to consider whether any developments of the past decade suggest that we need to modify our objectives or our methods of reaching them, and to pinpoint the areas where further study is required to define our course.

2.   I believe that the Report achieves these objectives and provides a sound basis on which to take decisions for the future. I am especially glad that, after considering particular aspects such as buildings, staff and finance, the Report goes on to consider the more general aspects of how to bring about change — the management and monitoring of services, the planning of co-ordinated new patterns of service and the roles of the voluntary and private sector. One of the most important changes of recent years has been the increasing part played by voluntary bodies and by informal groups of parents and friends, in helping the local community to become more aware of mentally handicapped people in their midst; for it is there, in the community, that most mentally handicapped people can lead as full a life as possible.

3.   The main conclusions of the Report are summarised in Chapter 10. I strongly endorse the final conclusion — that we need to build a pattern of local services and that for this the basic principles of the 1971 White Paper hold good. These principles have recently been re-stated in the Model of Care set out in the Report of the Committee chaired by Mrs Peggy Jay. In the present economic situation we shall not be able to make progress as fast as we would all like. But we must use the resources available to build, as quickly and ingeniously as we can, the services needed.

4.   There is now good advice to help in planning better provision for the mentally handicapped. The broad strategy is set out in the 1971 White Paper as modified in this Review and, linked with it, the Jay Committee's 'Model of Care'. Guidance on the setting up of services is available in the publications of

the National Development Group, and in an increasing number of publications about the way in which particular authorities are tackling the task in their locality. There remain some aspects — such as the care of the multiply handicapped — on which more will need to be done.

5.   The National Development Group have also provided authorities and others with a Checklist, which has recently been published. The Checklist will help authorities to monitor their current services and to evaluate the services they are planning for the future. Finally, the Development Team for the Mentally Handicapped will continue to be available to assist individual health and social service authorities; the Team's general Reports, of which two have so far been published, draw together the main findings from their visits.

6.   The basic principles on which we should work are clear — in brief, that of recognising the rightful place of mentally handicapped people, in our communities and of making services available accordingly. Given that framework, the detailed provision of services within the statutory and voluntary resources available should be for the local community and its authorities to decide. In doing so, they will need to study carefully lessons learnt elsewhere, and the ideas of those with special experience in this field. It is my hope that, across the country, we can sustain and build on the progress that has been made in raising the quality of life of a group of people who have to face life with a grievous handicap. They deserve our help, our support and above all our continuing concern.

PATRICK JENKIN

December 1980   Secretary of State for Social Services

Table of Contents   Page

Chapter 1 Introduction

1.1   Nine years ago, the Government of the day published a White Paper "Better Services for the Mentally Handicapped". It set the course which it was believed policy on services for mentally handicapped people should follow into the early 1990s, and it specified planning targets which it was hoped authorities could achieve by that date. The main recommendations concerned the development of co-ordinated health and personal social services for mentally handicapped people in each locality, a major shift in responsibility for the residential care of mentally handicapped people from health to local authorities, involving a considerable increase in local authority provision, and a considerable increase in adult training centre provision.

1.2   In 1978 the previous Secretary of State decided that the time had come to take stock of progress so far, and to consider whether any changes to the guidance set out in the White Paper might be needed. The present Secretary of State confirmed that the review should continue. Indeed the current constraints on public expenditure make it more rather than less important to consider the achievements of authorities so far, to reassess the feasibility of the White Paper programme and to consider how the principles underlying the White Paper can best be translated into practical policies for the fore-seeable future.

1.3   Taking stock is not just a question of looking at progress towards implementing the policies in the White Paper. It is also important to consider new ideas and developments, some reflecting advances in knowledge of how the effects of mental handicap can be alleviated and advances in the investigation and treatment of associated handicaps, others representing practical alternatives to existing patterns of service. Many of these have come about as a result of initiatives by people actively engaged in providing a service to mentally handicapped people. Fresh insights have come, too, from research. The work in the National Development Group for the Mentally Handicapped, the Development Team for the Mentally Handicapped and the Committee of Enquiry into Mental Handicap Nursing and Care (the Jay Committee), have led to the widespread dissemination of new ideas from these and other sources.

1.4   In this country there has been a greater political emphasis in recent years on the needs of deprived and handicapped people, leading to priority being given by successive Governments to the development of services for these groups.

1.5   On the debit side, aspects of the care given to mentally handicapped people have continued to give cause for concern. Public inquiries into NHS hospitals have tended to attract most publicity, but local authority, voluntary and private services have also been the object of criticism.

1.6   Finally, assumptions in the White Paper about public expenditure have proved to be unreaslistic. The White Paper was written at a time of expansion. Since then restraints in public spending have meant that authorities could not progress as rapidly as was originally hoped, despite the priority which successive Governments have continued to attach to the development of mental handicap services. At the present time, there seems little prospect of an early end to such restraints.

1.7   In this document the team of officials who have been carrying out the review with the assistance of Professor Peter Mittler, Chairman of the National Development Group for the Mentally Handicapped, set out what they see as the salient facts about mental handicap services as they exist at present and as they have been developing over recent years and draw some conclusions from them. We drew mainly on national statistics and other sources of information already available within the Department of Health and Social Security. However, we also commissioned operational research studies and sought additional information from five Case Registers (to which further reference is made in Chapter 3), and are indebted to Mrs Denise McKnight for early sight and discussion of a review of literature on various aspects of mental handicap services which had been commissioned by the DHSS during the period of our study. Our conclusions are of two kinds. They include, firstly, ideas about what can be done in the short term to maintain the existing position and, where possible, continue to make progress in the direction of White Paper principles and, secondly, views on the problems which will have to be tackled in the longer term if further progress is to be made towards a pattern of services more closely related to the principles set out in the White Paper (Appendix A).

1.8   We have taken the opportunity to discuss each of these principles and their continuing relevance. We consider that, whilst some of them might nowadays be expressed in a different way, they remain a sound basis on which to plan the development of better services for mentally handicapped people. But the principles do not lay sufficient stress on the role of parents, and there might be scope for additional principles suggesting that a choice of services should be made available where possible and that, where possible, mentally handicapped people ought to be given a part in making decisions affecting them personally.

1.9   In Chapter 2 we describe the services available to mentally handicapped people as they have developed since the White Paper. In Chapter 3 we set out information on the numbers and characteristics of mentally handicapped people, and refer to the special needs of certain groups of mentally handicapped people. Chapter 4 looks at the size of facilities for mentally handicapped people. Chapter 5 is about the major resource provided

— staff, and Chapter 6 is about finance. In Chapter 7 we discuss the management and monitoring of services, turning to planning in Chapter 8. Chapter 9 refers to the important role of the voluntary and private sectors. Finally, in Chapter 10, we summarise the salient points arising from the previous chapters and make some suggestions both for short-term action and on issues requiring long-term consideration.

Chapter 2   Services for Mentally Handicapped People

Legislation

2.1   In this chapter we take a broad look at the services which are provided today and how they have developed since the publication of the White Paper in 1971. We begin with a brief discussion of the statutory framework. The main pieces of legislation which affect mentally handicapped people are listed in Appendix B.

2.2   There is a striking difference between the legislation relating to health services and that relating to social services, particularly when account is taken of regulations and directions. Health authorities provide services under the general powers in the National Health Service Act 1977, whereas local authorities have been given far more explicit duties and powers, either in the primary legislation (eg the Chronically Sick and Disabled Persons Act 1970) or through the Ministerial directions contained in LA Circulars 13/74 and 19/74. Legislation and directions say little, however, about the quantity and quality of any type of service which either health or local authorities should provide.

2.3   This situation reflects the different relationships between the Secretary of State and the two types of authority. The National Health Service Act lays the duties to provide health services on the Secretary of State. Although he has delegated many functions to health authorities they remain directly accountable to him. There are therefore fewer specific legislative powers and duties than there are in the case of social services where the responsibility lies with individual local authorities.

2.4   It is also noticeable that no legislation affects only services for the mentally handicapped. Whether this should continue to be the case is at present a subject of debate in the context of the review of the Mental Health Act 1959. The fact that legislation is spread among a number of Acts which in their turn may refer to circulars and regulations may lead to confusion. But on the other hand, the linking of legislation affecting mental handicap services with legislation on other services is in line with the policy that services for the mentally handicapped should develop as part of the general health and personal social services.

Guidance

2.5   We have referred to two circulars which contain directions having legal force. Most circulars issued by DHSS are, of course, not of this kind and contain guidance rather than instructions for field authorities. A list of the guidance circulars which have most relevance to mental handicap services is at Appendix C. It will be seen that in contrast to the legislative provisions but again reflecting the Secretary of State's more direct responsibility for the health service, more and more detailed guidance has been provided to health than to local authorities. In the mental handicap field, of course, the main source of guidance is the 1971 White Paper, which covered both health and local authority services.

Services for mentally handicapped people living in the community

2.6   Most mentally handicapped people live with their own families or independently. It has been estimated that up to nine-tenths of severely mentally handicapped children now live at home. The proportion receiving residential care in staffed accommodation increases with age, and some three-fifths of severely mentally handicapped adults live in hospitals or residential homes. Many are placed in hospitals who could be in other forms of residential care, or in hostels and housing where supporting staff come in. Good community services can both improve the quality of life for mentally handicapped people already in the community and their families and help to ensure that only those individuals whose needs are best met in that way are admitted to residential care.

Living independently

2.7   Mentally handicapped people capable of renting accommodation of their own have the same rights to do so as other people. Domiciliary support and perhaps some minor adaptation of the dwelling may be needed so that they can run a home on their own or sharing with other people. In the short term a hostel place can help adjustment to independent living by those moving from the family home or elsewhere. For those who will always need some support there is the possibility of using subsidised housing accommodation where staff or volunteers come in from outside where needed, or give cover on a shift basis. Already a number of housing authorities, housing associations and new town development corporations have arrangements with local social services departments, and voluntary organisations, by which the housing needs of mentally handicapped people are met. The way that care is provided and the management style will however determine whether a scheme will benefit from housing subsidy. The Housing Corporation has issued guidance to housing associations on this subject. Health and social services authorities remain responsible for funding the provision of accommodation for those who require a high degree of care and support (though that does not rule out their purchasing or renting housing if this is seen as the appropriate way to care for their clientele).

Generic health and personal social services

2.8   Like everyone else, mentally handicapped people are entitled to receive primary health and social care from the "generic services" (general community-based services as opposed to specialist services for mentally handicapped people) provided by general practitioners, health visitors, dentists, social workers, home helps and others. They are also entitled to help and treatment from opticians, chiropodists, speech therapists, occupational therapists and other members of the professions supplementary to medicine. In addition, they are also entitled to any specialist treatment required for physical disorders. Mentally handicapped children attending school will of course receive attention from the school health service in the same way as other children.

2.9   There is little information available about the extent to which mentally handicapped people benefit from "generic services" or the degree of priority given to them. When studies of community care are reported they have been disquieting and suggest that many families are not receiving the help they need. Social work and primary health care agencies are fully stretched and have to decide priorities amongst many competing claims and 'at risk' cases, according to an assessment of local and individual needs. Most professionals working in the community will individually come across relatively few mentally handicapped people. In these circumstances it can be difficult for a person who has little experience of mentally handicapped people or training on this subject to appreciate the kind of development which might be possible, or the sort of help which would be most effective. Multidisciplinary post-experience courses can help to make people more aware of the needs of the mentally handicapped and where to turn for help, but no more.

Specialist staff in the community
2.10   In response to these problems, demand has grown for staff who can both offer support, guidance and specialised knowledge to colleagues in their own and other disciplines on the particular problems of mental handicap and also work with mentally handicapped people and their families, especially those with the most severe difficulties.

2.11   Some social services departments have made appointments, often under joint financing, of specialist social workers for mentally handicapped people. These may be based in hospital, in the local authority social services department or operate as part of the community mental handicap team. Their functions usually include intensive casework support to families of mentally handicapped people, providing information on resources, and participating in multidisciplinary assessment and treatment planning. They also act as sources of advice to colleagues with a less detailed knowledge of mental handicap and its problems. On the health side, an increasing number of mental handicap nurses are working in the community. In 1977 an estimated 135 (54 wte)* mental handicap nurses based in hospitals were involved in visiting mentally handicapped people at home out of an estimated total of 563 (229 wte) involved in activities other than services for residents in the hospital in which they are based (eg out-patient clinics). The amount of time each nurse spends working in the community will vary from nurse to nurse and from district to district.

*Wte = Whole-time equivalent

6

Recent Developments

2.12 Specialist services for mentally handicapped people living at home and for their families are still in their infancy. There has been little central guidance on the sort of services which should be provided, and authorities have tackled the recognised need for such services in a number of different ways. In the following paragraphs we describe briefly some ideas which have come to the attention of the Department.

2.13 A number of authorities provide (or are planning to provide) specialist advice and help through interdisciplinary Community Mental Handicap Teams, consisting of both NHS and local authority staff. They can also act as a source of expert advice to staff providing a generic service, offer specialised help to people in local residential and day care and help to establish a close working relationship with local voluntary organisations. The National Development Group for the Mentally Handicapped commended the setting up of such teams in their pamphlet "Mentally Handicapped Children: A Plan for Action", and a further description of the possible help such teams can give can be found in the First Report of the Development Team for the Mentally Handicapped.

2.14 The Development Team has also suggested the setting up of Community Units. Such units could provide a base for the community team, observation and assessment facilities for adults and children, programmes of teaching in simple skills for mentally handicapped people living at home (including teaching parents to carry out programmes at home), physiotherapy, speech therapy and other similar services on a sessional basis, short term residential care, a centre for parent and voluntary activity and a centre for consultation between professionals.

2.15 Another (not necessarily alternative) suggestion which is being considered in some places is to nominate a 'named person' for every mentally handicapped person to provide a single point of contact for his family, to act as a source of advice and to ensure access to other agencies and services. Such a person might be a social worker or a Community Mental Handicap Nurse or could come from one of the other agencies in contact with the family.

2.16 Many authorities have also found it useful to have a resource bank of information on facilities and services in the area, and to issue and keep up-to-date a basic list available both to parents and to health and care agencies in the area including local voluntary organisations. This might include information on social security benefits, grants, where to go for help with housing or employment, and local voluntary organisations who might be able to provide various kinds of assistance.

Education

2.17 Mentally handicapped children have the same right as all other children to receive education provided by local education authorities. The present review excludes consideration of educational matters, but close co-operation between health, social services and education authorities is essential both whilst a child is at school and at the important time of transition from school to adult life. Some information about educational provision is given in Appendix D. The whole range of special education, from the earliest years to adulthood, was reviewed by the Committee of Inquiry into the Education of Handicapped Children and Young People (the Warnock Committee) whose Report was published in 1978. The Committee's conclusions and recommendations have been widely endorsed and the Government announced in March that it intends to introduce legislation to enact a new framework for special education substantially on the lines proposed by the Committee. A White Paper outlining the proposed legislation and dealing with other recommendations made in the Report has been published.

2.18   The value of pre-school educational activities, and of involving parents in the education of their children, is increasingly being recognised and the Warnock Committee identified the further development of educational and associated services for children under five as particularly important. Research teams in Wessex and Cardiff have been looking at ways of developing skills by the use of a home teaching service for families with a pre-school mentally handicapped child. Under the supervision of a strong management team home teachers — in both places staff from a variety of backgrounds have been used with equal success — teach parents to use the Portage developmental checklist of behavioural skills to develop different skills in pre-school children. The Hester Adrian Research Centre at Manchester has also been studying a variety of ways in which parents can be brought more fully into partnership with professionals and be helped to develop a teaching role with their child.

2.19   Some mentally handicapped young people stay on at school beyond 16. An increasing number of local education authorities provide a range of opportunities in further education establishments for mentally handicapped young people and adults, including link courses with special schools and day release from adult training centres. A few provide full-time special courses usually of one or two years' duration. Many LEAs also provide teachers to work in adult training centres and/or a teaching service in mental handicap hospitals, sometimes linked with the hospital special school but more usually with the further education of adult education services. The Warnock Report looked forward to an extension of these developments.

Work
2.20   On leaving school, most young people hope to start work. Placement in open or sheltered employment is possible for many mildly mentally handicapped people and some of the more severely handicapped. The Manpower Services Commission has responsibility for policy on the operation of all the main services concerned with the employment, rehabilitation and training of disabled people though young disabled people look primarily to the local authority careers service for guidance and placement. The services offered by these bodies are briefly outlined in Appendix E and include a number of schemes which can help to establish mentally handicapped people in employment. Unfortunately, few severely handicapped people seem to get access to these services. Mentally handicapped people nearly always require

help in finding a job and thereafter, but when unemployment is relatively high, particularly amongst young people, such help is even more essential and the numbers of mentally handicapped people able to obtain jobs will in any event fall. We refer to the impact that the lack of employment opportunities can have on adult training centres later.

Adult Training Centres

2.21 Some mentally handicapped school leavers will not be ready to start work, and others particularly the more severely handicapped, may never reach that stage. All, however, will require positive and worthwhile daytime activity. Local authority adult training centres provide a wide range of activities for an increasing number of mentally handicapped people of all levels of ability. The major source of information we have about the characteristics of trainees in adult training centres comes from the survey carried out by Edward Whelan and Barbara Speake in 1973-4. The information is limited, but highlights the youth of the trainees. Nearly two-thirds were under 30, and less than a tenth over 50. 80% were living in the family home and 13% lived in hostels.

2.22 The White Paper called for a substantial expansion in the number of adult training centre places. Table 2.1 shows the progress made so far.

Table 2.1 Adult Training Centre Places   England

	Provided 1969	Provided 1977	1991 White Paper Target*
Numbers	23,200	38,700	74,900
Rate per 100,000 population aged 16+	67	110	202

Nearly all local authorities have at least one ATC, but the number of places provided varies widely, with the South-East of England generally having well below half the number of places the White Paper said would be needed by 1991 while some local authorities, particularly in the North, are already approaching the White Paper target level.

Daytime activities in hospital

2.23 Most people living in mental handicap hospitals undertake daytime activities arranged by the hospital, though a few (under 800 on one day in 1977) attend adult training centres. Table 2.2 shows the activities undertaken by mental handicap hospital residents on the first full working day of November 1977.

2.24 A small number of people living outside hospitals attend a hospital for day services (some 870 on one day in 1977). This figure relates only to adults. A few children attend hospital schools on a daily basis, but health authorities should no longer be providing day services for children of school age on a regular basis, though they may provide day care at weekends and during school holidays.

Residential Care

2.25   The White Paper set targets for 1991 for hospital places and for places in residential homes (including local authority, voluntary and private accommodation in the latter). In each case, it distinguished between places for children and those for adults. In the following paragraphs we look first at the provision made for children and then at that made for adults.

The White Paper targets have been updated to take account of projected changes in the population as a whole by 1991 and the rate of provision has been expressed in respect of the age appropriate population rather than the population as a whole. This is because (a) the age distribution of the population varies from place to place and local planners will have to take account of this, (b) the age distribution of the population varies over time, thus affecting the updated White Paper targets.

TABLE 2.2   **Daytime Activities of Mental Handicap Hospital Residents 1977**   England

	Number participating	% of residents
Industrial	8,521	17.7
Handicrafts	9,709	20.2
Social Training	7,976	16.6
Hospital Service Departments	4,439	9.2
Outside Job	837	1.7
Full-time education[1]	5,922	12.4
Other	3,026	6.3
Total[2]	35,904	74.7

[1]All ages. Figure includes those attending ATCs.

[2]For this calculation a resident has only been counted once against his major employment, although he may have more than one occupation during the day.

Residential Services for Children

2.26   Table 2.3 shows how the number of children in mental handicap hospitals and units has been falling over the years to well below the level envisaged in the White Paper. The excess of the White Paper target for 1991 over the current level of usage is not quite as great as the figures at first sight suggest, since the 1969 and 1971 figures are numbers of children whereas the 1991 target is in terms of *places* for children. Nonetheless it is clear that the White Paper target is substantially over-generous.

TABLE 2.3   **Children in Mental Handicap Hospitals and Units**   England

	Children aged 0–15		1991 White Paper Target* for Children's Places
	1969	1977	
Numbers	7,100	3,900	5,200
Rate per 100,000 population aged 0–15	62	35	53

10

The number of children has gone down by about 350 a year since 1969 compared with a decrease of only 100 a year between 1963 and 1969. These national figures conceal substantial variation between Regions, from NE Thames with only 24 children in hospital per 100,000 population aged 0–15 and North Western with 26 to SW Thames with 73 and Wessex with 46 per 100,000.

2.27   The White Paper pointed to a gross shortage of residential homes for mentally handicapped children and called for a substantial increase in provision. The growth of the number of places in such homes has been disappointingly small, as Table 2.4 shows, though the figures are affected by an unexpected apparent fall in the number of places by 300 between 1970 and 1972. This may have resulted from some establishments changing their registration to education authorities following the Education (Handicapped Children) Act 1970. Appendix D suggests that some 800 severely handicapped children attend boarding schools.

TABLE 2.4   Places in Residential Homes for Mentally Handicapped Children   England

	Provided 1969	Provided 1977	1991 White Paper Target*
In LA homes	1,200	1,600	Not specified
In all homes	1,700	2,200	4,000
Rate per 100,000 population aged 0–15	15	20	40

*See page 10.

Provision is very variable, with 40 out of 109 local authorities still providing no places of their own, of whom 20 provide none from any source in homes specifically designated for mentally handicapped children. The South East generally is more than half way towards meeting White Paper targets, while the North East has not yet reached a third of those levels.

Residential Services for Adults
2.28   Table 2.5 shows that the number of adults in mental handicap hospitals and units has gone down by over 600 a year since 1969. This can be compared with a slight *increase* between 1963 and 1969. However, the fall has not been as rapid as anticipated at the time of the White Paper.

TABLE 2.5   Adults in Mental Handicap Hospitals and Units   England

	Adults aged 16+		1991 White Paper target*
	1969	1977	
Number	49,200	44,100	27,300
Rate per 100,000 population aged 16+	142	125	74

As in the case of children, there are marked differences between Regions, from 89 adult hospital residents per 100,000 population aged 16 and over in NE Thames and 92 in Mersey to 244 per 100,000 in SW Thames and 173 in South Western. There are still 85 out of 205 health Districts with no mental handicap beds at all, and 94% of all mental handicap beds are in the 70 Districts which provide 200 or more beds.

2.29   Table 2.6 indicates progress made in providing places in residential homes for mentally handicapped adults.

TABLE 2.6   Places in Residential Homes for Mentally Handicapped Adults   England

	Provided 1969	Provided 1977	1991 White Paper target*
In LA homes	3,100	8,100	Not specified
In all homes	4,200	11,700	30,000
Rate per 100,000	12	33	81

*See page 10.

There is again substantial geographical variation with authorities in the Midlands less than a third of the way towards the levels of provision envisaged in the White Paper and those in the North West more than half way there.

The Balance of Care

2.30   Figure 2.1 shows in graphic form the changes which the White Paper envisaged would take place in the balance of care between hospitals and residential homes and the progress made up to 1977. The top row refers to provision for adults and the bottom row to provision for children. In each case the charts show the position in 1969, the position in 1977 and the White Paper's proposals for 1991. In looking at these charts, it should be borne in mind that the 1977 charts relate to a year roughly one-third of the way between 1969 and 1991, and that the size of the circle represents the total number of places.

2.31   The massive shift away from hospital care proposed by the White Paper (and the great task thereby laid on local authorities) is immediately apparent. But there are other points worth noting too. In particular, it can be seen that, if places in hospitals and residential homes are added together, the White Paper envisaged that the number of places for adults would remain about the same even though the distribution of those places between hospitals and homes would be very different. Furthermore, it will be seen that the total number of places in 1977 is in line with this. On the children's side, however, the White Paper envisaged a small increase in the number of places whereas what in fact has happened is that the number of places has fallen, because of the rapid fall in the number of children in hospitals. It seems likely that local authority services will in future constitute a higher proportion of the places provided than the White Paper envisaged. It is also worth adding a reminder

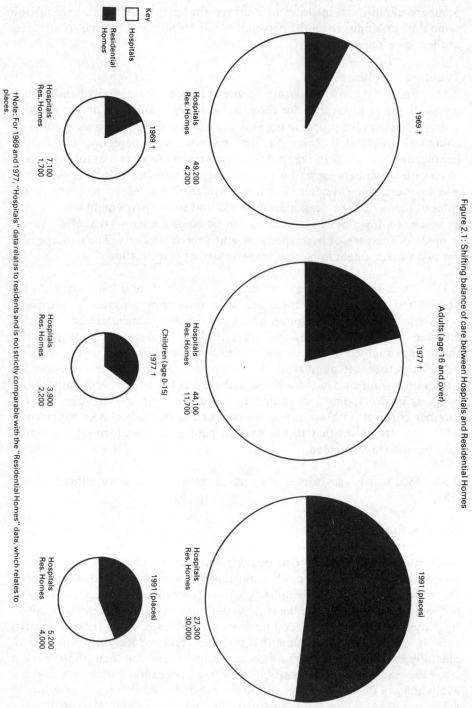

Figure 2.1: Shifting balance of care between Hospitals and Residential Homes

Adults (age 16 and over)

1969 †

Hospitals	49,200
Res. Homes	4,200

1977 †

Hospitals	44,100
Res. Homes	11,700

1991 (places)

Hospitals	27,300
Res. Homes	30,000

Children (age 0-15)

1969 †

Hospitals	7,100
Res. Homes	1,700

1977 †

Hospitals	3,900
Res. Homes	2,200

1991 (places)

Hospitals	5,200
Res. Homes	4,000

Key

■ Hospitals
□ Residential Homes

†Note: For 1969 and 1977, "Hospitals" data relates to residents and is not strictly comparable with the "Residential Homes" data, which relates to places.

13

here that this shift of care was not expected to be accompanied by an equivalent shift in finance. Expenditure on the health service was expected to continue to increase for some considerable time, though at a reducing rate as numbers diminished, in order to improve the quality of health care: at the same time expenditure on the personal social services would need to increase, as these developed.

Tentative conclusions

2.32   Far less is known about the services provided for mentally handicapped people living at home than for those in hospitals, residential homes and day settings. Services for people living at home are central to a successful policy of community-orientated care. Studies of the way parents of mentally handicapped people perceive their need for services suggest that there is a lack of co-ordination between and within the various agencies leading both to gaps and to overlapping services. Further consideration needs to be given to the roles of the various professionals involved and to the part volunteers can play as well as to how services to families can be co-ordinated so that effective use is made of the time of both specialist and generic workers. The concept of a 'named person' might in particular merit further investigation.

2.33   On residential and day services, the broad picture is fairly clear. As far as children are concerned there has been only slow progress in providing residential care outside hospital, whilst the number of mentally handicapped children in hospital has fallen dramatically. As a result, instead of an increasing number of places for children taking hospitals and residential homes together, the number of children in one or other form of residential provision has fallen. On the adult side there has been reasonably satisfactory progress in developing local authority residential and day services, but the number of people in hospital has not declined as fast as had been expected in 1971 and this means that the number of people in some form of residential care has actually increased.

2.34   Whilst it is easy to see what has happened, it is more difficult to say why.

Services for Children

2.35   It is particularly difficult to understand the changes which have taken place in children's services. One possible explanation, of course, is that better services to families with mentally handicapped children have reduced the need for residential care. The emphasis of both health and social services is increasingly on maintaining the child within his own family wherever possible, by providing practical help, counselling and periods of short-term residential care. It is reasonable to assume that the availability of support to parents of mentally handicapped children at home, improvements in education services since the assumption of responsibility by local education authorities, and the availability of flexible short-term care for periods ranging from a few hours to a few days can reduce the need for residential care. Where placement away from home becomes necessary, one alternative is to find a substitute (foster or adoptive) family for either short-term or long-term care, though it is not easy

14

to find substitute parents for mentally handicapped children and at present very few children are being cared for in this way.

2.36 The attitudes of families with mentally handicapped children to residential care may also have changed for other reasons. For example, the provision of social security benefits such as Attendance Allowance and Mobility Allowance may have helped families to keep their handicapped child at home, and changing attitudes in the community at large may also have encouraged them to do so.

2.37 We know that some mentally handicapped children are now being provided for in places such as foster or adoptive homes, ordinary children's homes, private nursing homes or hospitals not specifically for the mentally handicapped, but we do not know how many because information about the presence of mentally handicapped children in such places is not collected centrally. We believe that the use of such alternatives to residential care as fostering and boarding out merits further consideration.

2.38 However, we do not believe the whole decline in the number of children in hospital can be attributed to reasons of this kind. There is evidence that some hospitals have decided that they will not admit children, particularly young children, under any circumstances, even though the unilateral withdrawal of NHS places without ensuring through joint planning that appropriate alternatives are available may place unacceptable burdens on families.

2.39 We must acknowledge at this point that the subject of hospital services for mentally handicapped children is a highly controversial one. Current Departmental policy is that some children do require long-term health care whilst others require long-term placement in a residential home. In either case the unit should be small, domestic in style and normally separate from provision for adults. Local authority provision, limited though it is, is generally in line with these criteria. However, a number of health authorities are planning long-stay provision for mentally handicapped children on the same site as that for adults, either in mental handicap hospitals or in District General Hospitals. It is argued that, where children and adults are cared for on the same site, this makes it possible for transition from children to adult units to be planned more flexibly on an individual basis and alleviates the problems associated with moving mentally handicapped adolescents from an environment where they feel at home to somewhere completely strange. Some would even favour mixed units of adults and children, arguing that these create a family atmosphere to the benefit of both. These points merit further consideration, but we believe the time has come to state unequivocally that large hospitals do not provide a favourable environment for a child to grow up in. District General Hospitals, whose main concern is acute medical treatment, are even more unsuitable than large mental handicap hospitals.

2.40 Some people would go further. A number of voluntary organisations have been pressing the Department to take a firm view that no mentally handicapped children should be in hospital on a long-term basis and that arrangements should be made for the discharge of all such children living in hospital as soon as possible. They believe that all mentally handicapped children can be cared for in some sort of very small unit. Many would agree with this with the proviso that some units might need to be run by the NHS rather than local authorities. In fact, awareness of these views and also of the standard of care received by some mentally handicapped children in hospital may be another cause of the fall in numbers as parents may have been discouraged from seeking hospital care for their children.

2.41   With such a wide divergence of views, further consideration clearly needs to be given to the pattern of services for children. However, on the facts at our disposal, we are clear that the White Paper target for hospital places for children was excessive. The number of children in hospital has fallen rapidly and it may well be that even the present national average of 35 places per 100,000 population aged 0–15 is higher than will ultimately be required. But we cannot tell how much further the figure will fall. We note that the Development Team in their first report stated that in their opinion about a quarter of the children in hospitals visited by them did not need long-term residential care of the kind they were receiving; in their latest report, they suggest that very few children are now being admitted to hospital for long-term care. Clearly, authorities should not plan in the longer term for more than 35 places per 100,000 population aged 0–15, though how fast longer-term targets can be attained must depend on the rate at which alternative provision can be built up. It must be a matter for local decision based on joint planning.

2.42   Poor progress on the provision of local authority residential provision for mentally handicapped children makes it impossible to quantify the long-term need. We consider that, for the time being, the local authority target should stand.

Services for Adults
2.43   As regards services for adults, the White paper advised that local authorities should concentrate first in preventing inappropriate admissions to hospital. It envisaged that after a while the demand from the community would be satisfied and that authorities could then turn to making provision for hospital residents thus speeding up the discharge of people inappropriately resident in hospital. There is no evidence that this is happening as yet. Hospitals often make their own arrangements for settling people in the community, for example by establishing their own hostel-type accommodation or group homes in property owned or rented by the NHS or rented by the occupants after arrangements concluded between the health authority and the housing authority or a housing association. Residents have also been discharged to private lodgings, though particular care is obviously necessary when this course is considered in order to ensure adequate support for the tenants. Mentally handicapped people living in unstaffed accommodation will often benefit from attendance at an adult training centre, but the 1973 survey showed that very few trainees came from such accommodation at that time, though the numbers may be a little higher now.

2.44   There seems to us to be no evidence at present to support or confute the White Paper assumption that the overall number of residential places should remain unchanged. There is no difficulty in filling residential places, but we have little evidence of the scale or nature of unmet demand though there is considerable evidence of inappropriately met demand. Furthermore, before suggesting any change in the overall number of places, careful consideration would have to be given to a number of factors including the possibility that some people now receiving residential care could in fact live in unstaffed accommodation if supporting services were available and possible changes in the lifespan of mentally handicapped people.

2.45   We believe that consideration ought to be given to whether greater use can be made of alternatives to expensive, staffed residential accommodation such as group homes, satellite housing (group homes for people who have left residential accommodation which enable them to maintain links with staff and residents at their previous home for as long as they wish), lodgings and ordinary housing.

2.46   But is the balance between hospital services and other residential services for adults right? Some light is thrown on the subject by Development Team analysis which indicate that between one-third and one half of present hospital residents are considered by the Team to be suitable for discharge either immediately or after some training. However, about one in five of these able residents are now elderly and could not humanely be expected to move from what has now, after many years' residence, become their home. Nevertheless, if the DT figures are anywhere near right, they confirm the need for a further substantial drop in the number of hospital places; only about 40%–50% of present residents were considered by the DT to warrant long-term residential care with high staffing ratios. Against this must be set the possible unmet need in the community. Waiting times for "urgent" admissions are higher in mental handicap hospitals than in any other type of hospital.

2.47   We think it likely that the White Paper over-estimated the number of hospital places which will eventually be required. We cannot quantify this, but we stress the importance of building up residential provision outside hospital and of finding ways of further reducing the number of people in hospital who do not need to be there.

Balance between Health and Local Authority Provision
2.48   In considering residential accommodation for both children and adults, we have so far taken for granted the assumption in the White Paper that there are some mentally handicapped people who need hospital care and a distinct group of others who need local authority or other similar residential care. This assumption cannot go unchallenged, particularly at a time when opinion is moving towards at least a common sort of building for all groups of mentally handicapped people who require residential care. Any distinction must therefore depend on whether different groups of clients need different skills which NHS and social services staff may possess. The Jay Committee

has challenged the assumption that different skills are required in the staff who provide direct care to residents, at least for the vast majority of mentally handicapped residents and it would therefore be desirable to give further thought to the balance between health and local authority provision. The possibility of joint health and local authority provision also merits further consideration.

Day Services

2.49   Where day care is concerned, we see no basis for revising the target for adult training centres at present. The comparative youth of trainees, and the finding of Whelan and Speake that few trainees move on to open or sheltered employment, whatever the reasons for this, suggests that a continued growth in the number of places available will be needed for some time simply to provide places for school leavers. Increased provision of residential care in the community for people who might in the past have been admitted to hospital or for people who previously were in large hospitals will also give rise to a need for more adult training centre places. It might be worth considering means of making more effective use of available ATC places, whether the age for entering training centres should remain relatively flexible, as it is at present, and what day provision should be made for elderly mentally handicapped people as these points could affect the number of places required.

2.50   With the present high level of unemployment authorities are coming under pressure to make adult training centre places available to more mildly handicapped people who, in more favourable times, might have found employment. The group most likely to be put forward are those who in addition to their intellectual handicap have behavioural or personality difficulties. Decisions on whether to admit this group rest with individual authorities but, if such pressures are acceded to, additional places will be required at considerable cost to public funds and new forms of service might have to be developed within ATCs. The regime of present ATCs is geared largely to the needs of the severely mentally handicapped. The incorporation of a large number of mildly mentally handicapped people, often with additional difficulties, could lead to frustration and consequent further behavioural problems for the more able group, possible exploitation and lack of staff attention for the less able group and problems of management, organisation and regime for the centre as a whole. The question of what services, if any, should be provided for mildly handicapped people, whether by social services departments, through the careers service, as part of the employment services, or in enclave schemes, certainly merits consideration, particularly if the long-term prospects for employment of this group remain poor.

2.51   A particular problem arises over day care for the most severely handicapped. The White Paper said that there was "scope for the development of special care units by local authorities and of day places in hospitals. In many cases it will be desirable for hospitals and local authorities to arrange joint provision of appropriate staff and contributions to the running costs". It is certainly true that the success of special care units in local authority centres can depend to a large part on the co-operation of health authorities in making staff available to provide support. It is possible that more severely handicapped people could be catered for in these units if the support of, for example, district nurses and community psychiatric nurses (mental handicap) was available to assist and advise clients and staff. The development of special care in schools has probably contributed to the reduction in the admission of children to hospital, and its absence when young people leave school may well be a reason why many are admitted to hospital at that time. The National Development Group for the Mentally Handicapped has recommended that all ATCs should include a special care section and many local authorities have been developing special care units in adult training centres, often with the help of joint finance which has made a substantial contribution in this field. Some however continue to regard the day care of the most severely handicapped as primarily a hospital responsibility. Often hospitals are too isolated to provide day care for people in their catchment area, and there may therefore be a need for NHS day provision if it is felt that some people require services which cannot be provided in an ATC. A clearer view from the centre on the division of responsibility could lead to a faster rate of progress on such services, by avoiding protracted disputes about responsibility.

Summary of Conclusions

2.52   On the basis of the evidence available to us we conclude that:

i   large hospitals of any kind do not provide a favourable environment for a child to grow up in (2.39)

ii   the White Paper target for hospital places for children was excessive. Authorities should not plan in the longer-term for more than 35 children's places per 100,000 population aged 0–15 (2.41)

iii   for the time being the long-term target for local authority residential accommodation for children should stand (2.42)

iv   there is no evidence at present to support or confute the White Paper assumption that the overall number of residential places for adults provided by the NHS, local autorities and other bodies should remain unchanged (2.44)

v   it is likely that the White paper over-estimated the number of hospital places for adults which will eventually be required (2.47)

vi   there is no basis at present for revising the White Paper target for adult training centre places (2.49).

2.53   We consider that further work is required on:

i   the roles of the various professionals who provide services to families of mentally handicapped people, the part volunteers can play and how services to families can best be co-ordinated (2.32)

ii   the use of alternatives to residential care for children such as fostering and boarding out (2.37)

iii   policy on services for mentally handicapped children (2.41)

iv   whether greater use can be made of group homes, satellite housing, lodgings or ordinary housing (2.45)

v   the balance between health and local authority and other similar residential provision (2.48)

vi   means of making more effective use of available adult training centres and what day provision should be made for elderly mentally handicapped people (2.49)

vii   the question of what day services, if any, should be provided for mildly mentally handicapped people, including the contribution of the careers and employment services (2.50)

viii the responsibility for day care for the most severely handicapped people and the extent to which additional support from health service could enable more such people to be catered for in special care units (2.51).

Chapter 3   The People who use the services

3.1   So far we have been looking at services without looking in detail at the numbers of people who need them and without making anything other than broad distinctions between the clients for whom they are provided. In this chapter we record what we have found about overall numbers and characteristics of mentally handicapped people and examine some of the implications for services. What mentally handicapped people have in common are a general intellectual functioning level which is significantly below average, and problems in adapting to normal behaviour patterns and achieving social skills. All of this may lead to the person needing specialised health and personal social services. Those who are grouped under this heading of mental handicap have widely varying intellectual, physical and behavioural characteristics, and the degree of severity of an individual's physical or behavioural problems may vary during his lifetime. There are several widely acknowledged definitions in use, and the more common of these are reproduced in Appendix F. Many people with severe mental handicap have physical disabilities as well, which are often severe; they find it more difficult than other people to compensate for even a minor physical disability.

3.2   Though mental handicap and mental illness are sometimes grouped together under the broad term "mental disorder", care must be taken to distinguish between them. Mental illness can occur at any time of life, and with treatment it can often be cured. Mental handicap is usually present from birth or soon after, and it cannot be cured in the same way, although, with the right sort of training, education and care, an improvement in the person's general development can be achieved. Some mentally handicapped people also suffer from mental illness.

3.3   The IQ test has been accepted for a long time as a crude indicator of intellectual ability. An IQ between 50 and 70 is often taken as showing mild mental handicap, and an IQ below 50 as indicating a severe grade. Taken on its own, however a low IQ does not necessarily mean that a person is mentally handicapped in the sense that he needs special services. IQ 70 is not a hard and fast borderline between handicapped and non-handicapped any more than IQ 50 is a hard and fast dividing line between mild and severe handicap. In such cases, the person's behaviour pattern and ability to adapt to a normal independent life must also be taken into consideration, and this will help determine whether or not he or she needs to use special mental handicap services.

3.4   Given these problems of definition, how can authorities assess the number of people needing mental handicap services? A starting point is existing clients, ie those receiving residential care, day care (for adults) and specialised education (for children) and those who, although not receiving these services, have been identified by the service providers and authorities as being in need of them and willing to accept them. Information on the numbers of people needing services but not receiving them is not collected by the Department's statistical services and we therefore asked for information from five of the Case Registers for the Mentally Handicapped.

3.5   These Registers record all people in a particular locality who have contacts with special services for the mentally handicapped. The smallest Register we consulted covers a population of 120 thousand, the largest 2.7 million, and the other three between $\frac{1}{4}$ and $\frac{1}{2}$ million each. We are grateful to the five Registers which we asked for help and would like to take this opportunity to thank them for their hard work. The Registers concerned and brief details about them are given in Appendix G.

3.6   It must be acknowledged that there is no generally acceptable definition of need, and that each authority is planning its provision will adopt the definition which it believes is most appropriate to the local circumstances. In this situation, the best that can be done is to state the definition which we agreed with the five Case Registers for the purpose of making estimates and recognise that authorities may use different assumptions. The definition used was as follows:

> "*Include: the following Mentally Handicapped People* as needing special services. All those now receiving full time residential care, ESN(S) schooling, day care, or if they are receiving none of these services, having some problems with ambulance, continence or behaviour and not able to feed, wash and dress themselves. [Or designated severely subnormal.]
>
> *Exclude: the following Mentally Handicapped People* as not in need of special services. *Children* in ESN(M) schools not covered by the above. *Adults* not covered by the above who are ambulant, continent, have no behavioural problems and can feed, wash and dress themselves. In general these clients have had no contact with the special services for many years except possibly for an occasional visit from a social worker."

3.7   This definition of need is not determined by existing provision alone but has been expanded to include some of those not currently receiving care.

It may marginally over-estimate need because incontinence etc does not by itself necessarily determine the need for special care, but it also underestimates need to some extent because children aged 0–4 were excluded for practical reasons. The prevalence of need has been calculated for the populations covered by the five Case Registers. These do not constitute a random sample, so we do not know how typical they are of the country as a whole. The main disadvantages of our approach are that:

a.   it does not acknowledge, even in principle, that some clients may be receiving care inappropriate to their needs;

b.   it does not tell us the proportion of clients who should be in the various forms of residential or day care.

Other mechanisms will have to be developed to determine the proportion of clients requiring each type of residential and/or day facility and to identify those who are receiving inappropriate care.

3.8   The average "prevalence of need", as defined above, in the populations covered by the Case Registers was 3.2 per thousand population with a range from 2.9 to 3.4 per thousand population (ie all the figures are within 10% of the average). Details of the individual Registers and their rates are given in Appendix G.

3.9   Our average estimate of 3.2 per thousand population is similar to that of 2.9 used in the 1971 White Paper, which drew on a special survey in one locality and on early results from two Case Registers covered by our study. A number of people have criticised the way the White Paper figure was arrived at, and have argued it should have:

a.   acknowledged that local factors may lead to considerable variation from a national average; and

b.   omitted children aged 0–4 from the calculation of prevalence as some of the Registers used then did not record it.

After discussion with epidemiologists and others concerned with assessing factors which may affect prevalence, we concluded that these criticisms are justified and that a single national prevalence rate is not appropriate. It has its uses for national planning but can be misleading for use at local level, particularly when assessing needs in small authorities, eg, those with a population of about 100,000 people. Even for populations as large as 500,000 people, a single national average figure may not be appropriate. This is the reason we have presented a prevalence range for use as a guideline.

3.10   The development of techniques for the diagnosis of handicapped fetuses could result in the birth of fewer handicapped children. A reduction in the numbers of infants suffering from conditions which are the result of damage in the womb (eg rubella), those which are genetic in origin (eg Down's Syndrome) and those which may be a combination of both (eg neural tube defects) could be achieved if resources were made available to increase the availability of preventive services in ante-natal care and provided such services were taken up and the parents accepted termination of the pregnancy as an alternative to the birth of a handicapped child. These resources must include the vital fields of staff training and research. Whilst we trust that advances in prevention will continue to be made, their impact on numbers needing services will inevitably be gradual, and is in any event impossible to quantify, given the complexities we have referred to.

3.11 Except for the question of population migration, on which Registers agree that prevalence will tend to be higher in localities which have lost population and lower in those which have gained, the information we have been able to collect on the reasons for local variations has not been sufficiently conclusive, or well corroborated, for us to pass it on with any degree of confidence. Because of the variations which have been found in local prevalence, health and local authorities are urged jointly to assess their needs. This should initially be on the numbers receiving services (including those receiving services outside the area) and those who have had contact with services in the past. Data from ESN(S) schools should be included in forward planning of adult services. However, planners should bear in mind that existing supply does not necessarily reflect demand or need. The number of places provided in residential and day services does not give a clear picture of the demand for places, nor does it show whether those using the services have been appropriately placed to meet their needs.

3.12 We make no recommendation as to whether more Case Registers should be set up. This is something which should be determined locally, taking account of the considerable cost involved and of the use to which it is intended the proposed Register should be put.

Disabilities Associated with Mental Handicap
3.13 The Development Team have let us analyse data which they have collected on about 10,000 hospital residents. We have done this in a way which shows the degree to which disabilities occur in hospital residents. It is hoped that this work will eventually be published. The disabilities which were reported by the Development Team relate to mobility, certain behavioural problems, continence, self-care, vision, hearing, speech and reading, writing and counting skills.

3.14 One of the most important results from this analysis is that it indicated that in the country as a whole there are some 15,000 residents in hospital who are recorded as fully mobile, with no behavioural problems, continent and able to feed, wash and dress themselves. In addition, about 3,000 residents are recorded as being mobile, continent and with no behavioural problems but not entirely capable of feeding, washing and dressing themselves.

3.15 The information available on the disabilities of mentally handicapped people who are not in hospital is unfortunately much more limited as we only have such data for Wessex, Sheffield and from the OPCS survey for the Jay Report (which was restricted to those in local authority residential care). The

OPCS survey showed that those in local authority residential care were mainly mobile (99%), not behaviourally disturbed (93%), continent (95%), and able to feed, wash and dress themselves (87%) and thus were similar to the most able group in hospital. The method adopted by OPCS for collecting these data does not, however, enable us to re-analyse them by the characteristics of individual clients as was done for hospital residents. Table 3.1 sets out the findings of the OPCS survey on hospital and LA residents in more detail.

TABLE 3.1 Disabilities of Mentally Handicapped Residents 1976

	Hospitals		Residential homes	
	Adult wards %	Children's wards* %	Adult homes %	Children's homes* %
Unable to walk by themselves (even using walking aids)	14	34	1	8
Unable to feed themselves	17	51	2	24
Unable to wash and dress themselves	52	79	13	44
Had behaviour problems	25	50	7	34
Singly or doubly incontinent at least twice a week during the day	26	61	2	22
Doubly incontinent at least twice a week during the day	19	55	2	15
Singly or doubly incontinent at least twice a week during the night	29	67	5	26
Doubly incontinent at least twice a week during the night	18	55	1	12
Blind (or partially sighted)	4	11	2	4
Deaf (and could not use a hearing aid)	4	5	2	3
Cerebral Palsy	13	28	4	10
Heart Condition	5	4	3	4
Respiratory Illness	6	10	5	17
Arthritis	2	0	1	0
Epilepsy (including controlled epileptics)	28	44	12	18
Had at least one epileptic fit in the previous month	10	18	4	8
Special Diet	8	9	3	4

Source: OPCS Survey for Jay Committee

*Children's units were defined as being wards or homes in which more than half of the residents were aged under 16.

3.16   For those living at home, we have even less information available, as only two Registers have been able to give us data on a comparable basis. However, they have indicated that about 10% of the severely incapacitated (ie those who are non-ambulant and/or incontinent and/or behaviourally disturbed) over the age of 45 were still living at home, whereas for the 16 to 44 age group the percentage was about 40%; over 70% of severely incapacitated children aged 5 to 15 live at home. If these figures are typical of England then there are about 5,000 severely handicapped adults living at home. This happens to correspond to about 10% of the residential places provided for adults. In contrast, about half of the residential accommodation provided is used by clients with slight or no recorded incapacities.

3.17   Authorities should make every effort to ensure that they know of all severely mentally handicapped people living at home and regularly examine the services being provided for them to ensure that they and their families are getting the help they need. In this context, the importance of effective communication and co-operation between different professionals and the different authorities is self-evident. Failure to pass on information can mean depriving a family of help they need.

Tentative Conclusions
3.18   In the preceding paragraphs we have set out what we know about the prevalence of additional handicaps, particularly among people at present in hospital, and about the extent to which these additional handicaps occur in combination. But what does this information imply for service provision?

3.19   All people receiving mental handicap services have some needs in common which those services should be designed to meet. We have seen, however, that such people do not constitute a homogeneous group. Where particular additional needs can be identified they present a challenge to the services, particularly as they may appear singly or in any of an almost infinite variety of combinations.

3.20   Perhaps because service planners find it easier to think of services in terms of groups of people rather than for individuals, attempts have been made to identify groups of mentally handicapped people who, for various reasons, might be thought to have special needs. Age is one criterion that has been used. We have referred in the previous chapter to services for children, but adolescents and the elderly may also have special needs. Other groups can be formed of people who lack certain specific abilities such as those with sensory handicaps, people with physical disabilities and people who cannot communicate. It has also been suggested that profoundly handicapped people, people with autism, and people with severely disordered behaviour might benefit from services provided specifically for them. Finally, people whose handicap has not been present since early childhood, for example people suffering from the results of head injuries whose level of intellectual functioning is very low and who therefore enter the mental handicap services, and mentally handicapped people who are also mentally ill may too have special needs.

3.21   Some of the difficulties inherent in the concept of groups of people with special needs are immediately apparent from this list. For example, the categories are clearly not discrete. It is quite possible to have a blind, disturbed adolescent or a physically handicapped, elderly mentally handicapped person suffering from mental illness. Assessment of individual needs is vital, not only when mental handicap is first suspected, but at regular intervals throughout life. Where children are concerned, the District Handicap Team will have an important role to play.

3.22   Special services are not, of course, synonymous with special units. It may be a question of ensuring that the person concerned receives help from specialist staff or that the staff who are involved in the day-to-day care of that person obtain guidance and help on how best to meet the special needs of that individual. Sometimes it may be necessary to ensure that appropriate aids are provided or that the place where the person lives is adapted to enable him to move around it more easily.

3.23   However, special units may be required for certain groups. Some people may need to spend some time in such units for a specific purpose such as assessment or a particular programme of treatment or training. This could be either as a resident or on a daily basis. Others may need to live permanently in such units, either for their own benefit or because they adversely affect the quality of life of those with whom they live.

3.24   These points may perhaps be clearer if they are illustrated in respect of one particular group. We have chosen people with severe behaviour disorder for this purpose, as this is a group for which some special provision is already made.

3.25   Firstly, it is clear that, while we have referred to people with severe behaviour disorder as a group, in fact they are extremely diverse in terms of age, handicap, type of anti-social behaviour and individual requirements.

3.26   Disorders of behaviour in the mentally handicapped range from petty recidivism which may be dealt with by the Courts to aggressive and destructive behaviour which may require admission to a special hospital for treatment under conditions of maximum security. Within this range will be mildly mentally handicapped people who have committed petty offences or more substantial offences against other people or property. Amongst those with severe mental handicap there are a few who may have episodes of disruptive and sometimes violent behaviour, who pose very difficult management problems.

3.27   Like other "groups", people with severe behaviour disorder may require special skills and characteristics from staff wherever they live. These range from basic qualities of character, such as calmness and the ability to work with unrewarding clients, to special skills both in controlling violent episodes and in attempting to change undesirable behaviour. Some of these may be things staff in any situation can learn from people with experience of problems of this kind. Others may be of a more specialised nature.

3.28   This illustrates a more general point. Any specialist skill requires experience to acquire and maintain. Where occasional advice to staff is what is required, then help from experts with experience of a particular problem and ways of dealing with it in a wide variety of settings may be not only sufficient but even better than experience limited in the main to a single establishment. But if more regular specialised help is required by any individual then it may be better for him or her to receive this in a special unit where all staff have opportunity to acquire the necessary skills.

3.29   Factors other than staff skills can influence the decision to set up a special unit for people with special needs. Segregation may be necessary for the benefit of the person concerned. For example, hyperactive people may benefit from being separated from people who need a lot of stimulation and, to move outside the field of behaviour disorder for a moment, blind people who are sensitive to sound may be better off segregated from people who make a lot of noise.

3.30   In other cases, people may require a special environment which is not compatible with good care for other groups of people. For example, those with behaviour disorder may need indestructible fittings, lockable rooms and escape-proof outdoor space. Others may need to be segregated from other people, or perhaps from certain other groups of people, in order to protect the lifestyle or, indeed, the safety of others. For example, some people with behaviour disorder destroy furniture, others may attack or bully those weaker than themselves. In such circumstances, the needs of others have to be carefully balanced against the needs of the individual, as grouping people with undesirable characteristics together may mean that these characteristics are reinforced, thus making it even more difficult to bring about improvements. Furthermore, special units for people with rare types of problems clearly cannot be provided in every District, so admission to a special unit may often put a strain on the resident's links with his family and home community.

3.31   In fact, almost every conceivable approach has been tried in the case of people with behaviour disorder, ranging from national units (special hospitals), through interim regional secure units and locked wards in hospitals to complete integration. As might be expected from what has been said above, none of these approaches has been wholly satisfactory, but in addition to the difficulties mentioned in previous paragraphs, some further disadvantages of special units have become apparent. Firstly, the existence of special units tends to make staff in ordinary units less willing to care for people with even mild disorders of behaviour. With a wide range of provision the opportunities for saying that somebody ought to be somewhere else are increased still further. Secondly, it has proved difficult to get people out of special provision once they have been admitted even if they no longer need to be there. For example, special hospital staff have great difficulty in finding hospitals which are willing to accept special hospital residents who no longer require the degree of security provided there. Clearly, further work is needed on all these matters.

Summary of Conclusions

3.32 Available information suggests that the number of people needing special mental handicap services may fall within the range 2.9 to 3.4 per 1000 population, but particular local circumstances may produce a rate either higher or lower than extremes quoted. (3.8–3.9).

3.33 Health and local authorities should co-operate with one another in assessing local need and in planning the types of services required, although the figures quoted here might serve as a general guideline. (3.11). They should pay particular attention to the needs of severely mentally handicapped people living at home and their families (3.17).

3.34 We think that consideration needs to be given to whether specialised services, and if so of what nature, are required within the mental handicap services for any or all of the following groups of mentally handicapped people:

i   adolescents

ii   the elderly

iii people with sensory handicaps

iv   people with physical disabilities

v   people who cannot communicate

vi   profoundly handicapped people

vii people with autism

viii people with severely disordered behaviour

ix   people suffering from the results of head injuries whose level of intellectual functioning is very low

x   people who are also mentally ill

and if so, in what form, and whether this list is comprehensive.

Chapter 4   The size of Hospitals, Homes and Adult Training Centres

4.1   So far we have looked at the overall number of places and at such information as there is on services for people with special needs. But the White Paper was not only concerned with overall numbers. It was concerned too with the pattern of services, and in particular it proposed that there should be a comprehensive range of services in each locality.

Hospitals

4.2   It is difficult to reconcile a policy of providing local services with the perpetuation of the existing large hospitals. While the White Paper did not suggest that the large hospitals should eventually be closed it did restrict new building to fewer than 200 beds as this was the maximum likely to be needed in any locality. It suggested, too, that many new hospitals would be considerably smaller. Some sections of opinion have cast doubts on the desirability of even 200 bedded hospitals. Nonetheless, it is clear that large hospitals will be with us for some time yet, and that the services provided within them will have to continue to be maintained and improved.

4.3   Table 4.1 shows the number of hospitals of various sizes in 1970 and 1976 and the way the total number of beds available was distributed between them. Figure 4.1 shows some of this information in graphic form.

4.4   In looking at these diagrams, it should be remembered that some small units are annexes of larger hospitals and that some large hospitals are made up of a number of small units.

4.5   Whilst there are quite a number of small units, just over half the places are still in hospitals with 500 or more beds and over three-quarters of places are in hospitals with 200 or more beds. Any shift in the distribution of beds since 1970 seems to have been largely as a result of the overall decline in numbers which has particularly affected the largest hospitals. We have looked at the information available about capital spending over the period 1967/68 to 1976/77, bearing in mind that we only have information about schemes which cost more than a specified level (which varied over the period in question). In general, it would seem that at the beginning of the period (in other words, before and immediately after the White Paper) there was a relatively large investment in hospitals of 200 to 499 beds. Later the emphasis seems to have

e home-like accommodation. Throughout the period
...g expenditure on hospitals of over 500 beds, reflecting the
...y authorities when confronted with the need to replace
...nt and upgrade wards in old, unsatisfactory hospitals. Such
...ay be done at the expense of providing accommodation more in
...ne current policy.

4.1   Mental Handicap Hospitals and Units — England

Size of Hospital or Unit	1970		1976	
	Number of Hospitals or Units	Number of Beds	Number of Hospitals or Units	Number of Beds
0–49 Beds	76	1,900	115	3,000
50–199 Beds	82	8,600	88	9,000
200–499 Beds	37	11,900	41	13,900
500–999 Beds	23	15,100	20	13,000
1000–1499 Beds	6	7,100	8	9,400
1500–1999 Beds	7	12,300	3	4,900
2000 and Over Beds	1	2,200	—	—
Total	232	59,200	275	53,100

Source: 1970 and 1976 SH3 Returns

Note: The difference between the sum of numbers of beds and the totals shown is due to rounding.

Local authority provision

4.6   While on the subject of size, we took a look at local authority provision, expecting to find much less variation there than in the NHS, and to find provision more in line with current policy as a lot more of it will have been provided since the White Paper.

4.7   The White Paper said that the normal maximum size of residential accommodation for adults should be 25 places, and, for children, 20 places, adding that many homes may be smaller. The White Paper did not give any advice about the size of adult training centres but the current Local Authority Building Note suggests that the number of places should normally be between 50 and 150. The National Development Group for the Mentally Handicapped has suggested that centres at the upper end of the size range would be more likely to be able to provide the wider training and education opportunities which adult training centres are now beginning to offer.

4.8   We found that over 40% of local authority residential homes for adults were larger than the maximum size recommended in the White Paper, though nearly all of these had between 25 and 32 places. Only 6 homes (out of 375) had over 40 places, and only 3 over 45.

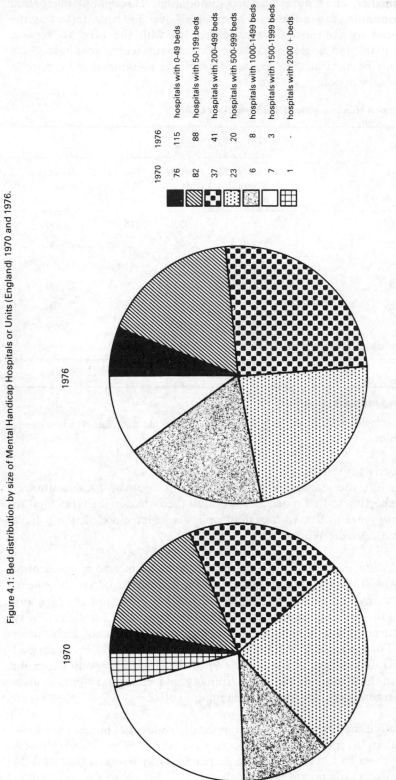

Figure 4.1: Bed distribution by size of Mental Handicap Hospitals or Units (England) 1970 and 1976.

	1970	1976	
■	76	115	hospitals with 0-49 beds
▨	82	88	hospitals with 50-199 beds
✚	37	41	hospitals with 200-499 beds
⬚	23	20	hospitals with 500-999 beds
▦	6	8	hospitals with 1000-1499 beds
☐	7	3	hospitals with 1500-1999 beds
▦	1	-	hospitals with 2000 + beds

4.9 The position as regards homes for children was rather different. Nearly half the homes had between 9 and 16 places and only 10% more than 24 places.

4.10 Over a quarter of adult training centres had less than 60 places, but only 6% had more than 160. Bearing in mind the National Development Group's preference for the upper end of the range, it is perhaps worth noting that only about a quarter of centres had more than 120 places.

Tentative conclusions

4.11 How important is size? There is a fair amount of evidence from research that the size of buildings is considerably less important for the quality of services than what goes on inside them. Services provided in any kind of building can and should be framed to meet the needs of the individual client, and staff in any kind of building can and should be assigned to small groups of clients. Thus, much can be done within existing stock to promote good services.

4.12 There are a number of arguments which can be put forward in favour of large units. Some people say that mentally handicapped people prefer the company of other handicapped people and are happier in an environment where they can remain all their lives and where they do not have to face the pressures of competing with people who are not handicapped. Concentrating relatively large numbers of mentally handicapped people on one site makes it easier to provide special leisure activities for them. A larger site allows more room for recreation and exercise which can be taken in safety without having, for instance, to cope with roads full of heavy traffic. It is argued that it is easier to make available the services of scarce specialists, such as speech therapists and physiotherapists, if mentally handicapped people are grouped together. Care staff can be more easily moved around if staff shortages occur in particular areas of the unit. Large units enable patients to be grouped according to their ability and moved more easily if they do not fit in to a particular ward. Staff feel less isolated than in a small unit where they may not be able to share problems with colleagues. Finally, it can be easier to administer services in a large unit, and problems such as transporting residents from their living accommodation to a distant training centre can be avoided.

4.13 However, given that, even taking the number forecast in the White Paper, few Districts are likely in the long term to need more than 150 or so NHS mental handicap beds in all, not all of which will be on one site, very large units are, in the long run, out of the question. Large units are very difficult to make homelike, even if built with that purpose in view, which is not the case with most of the hospitals we have inherited. Any very large facility will also tend to draw some of those it serves from so far away as to pose substantial problems of transport and community contact.

4.14 There is now some preliminary evidence from research in Wessex to support the view that it is no more difficult to hire staff for small units than for large ones, and that there can be greater continuity of staffing than in traditional hospitals. The Wessex research also indicates that contacts with "scarce" professionals need not be fewer in small units and that on various indices the "quality of life" provided can be at least as high as in large hospitals. All this tends to support commonsense assumptions that direct care staff are likely to be easier to recruit to dispersed facilities which minimise travelling time or the need to "live in", that "scarce" professionals may be more readily obtainable for sessions in local establishments which allow services to mentally handicapped people to be combined with other duties than for full-time service in isolated hospitals, and that unit size as such is not a determinant of the quality of care.

4.15   It has been suggested that it would not be possible to organise nurse training effectively in a service based on small units. The whole question of the training of staff working in the residential care of the mentally handicapped is, at the time of writing, under consideration in the context of the government's response to the report of the Committee of Enquiry into Mental Handicap Nursing and Care (the Jay Committee). However, it is our understanding that the General Nursing Council consider that it would be quite possible to organise nurse training in a service based on small units.

4.16   The Department has often been told by authorities that they believe that small units are more expensive to run than large hospitals. We have looked at the information available from returns submitted to the DHSS. The general pattern is that costs per resident increase with size up to 500 beds and then decline somewhat, though units up to 50 beds are still cheaper to run than the largest hospitals. But the variation in unit cost between individual hospitals of the same sort of size is very great. Research results from Wessex indicate that the costs of 5 small units there, 4 for very severely handicapped children and one for very severely handicapped adults, are broadly similar to those of local mental handicap hospitals. As to capital costs, it seems likely that building a small unit from scratch is rather more expensive per place than building a larger one of 100 beds or more. But in many cases existing property can be converted at far lower cost — we know of instances as varied as small cottage hospitals or maternity units, old rectories and council and other houses being adapted for use by mentally handicapped residents.

4.17   Further examination is needed of the question whether there is an optimum range of sizes for units of different kinds, given the over-riding need for ease of access to the population served and the requirement that any residential accommodation should be home-like in character. Further work is also required on whether it is better to provide a number of small units on a single site, or whether it will best serve the needs of residents for community contact and home-like surroundings if residential accommodation is provided on a number of separate sites, with day services separated from the living units and perhaps serving several of these. Such work would need to include consideration of the appropriate division of responsibility between health and social services, the implications for staff training and proper financial appraisal.

4.18 However, in the meantime we are convinced that health authorities contemplating new buildings for the mentally handicapped over the next few years should "think small". We believe there is no District in which it would not be useful to have at least one small health service unit. This might be, for example, a base for community services with some provision for assessment, day and short-term care, a small residential unit or a community unit as suggested by the Development Team. Before deciding on capital investment in an existing facility both health and local authorities need to consider carefully whether it would be preferable to cater for the clients off the site of the hospital. It may be as expensive to upgrade existing run-down wards as to supply a new small unit away from the hospital, either by new building or by adapting existing property such as houses or small hospitals no longer required for other purposes.

4.19 We appreciate that authorities do face a real dilemma here. Maintaining existing facilities until replacement facilities can be provided is expensive. Furthermore, where the facility being replaced is a large hospital, there may well be a long period of overlap during which replacement facilities are being built up but only limited savings are possible in the running costs of the hospital. There are also considerable difficulties as to planning and financing a transfer from a hospital run by a single health authority to a network of services run by a number of different health and local authorities. We return to these difficulties in other chapters.

4.20 The White Paper and subsequent publications have given clear guidance on the size of local authority facilities, and though, as we have shown, it has not been followed to the letter everywhere, the divergencies are not so substantial to cause us any real concern.

4.21 So far as the size of adult training centres is concerned, there are strong arguments in favour of large centres as these are able to provide a wider range of activities and more specialist staff than is possible in a small centre. However, large centres may be impractical in rural areas due to problems such as the time taken by long journeys. Indeed, the whole question of whether urban and rural areas may require different patterns of service is one which we have not been able to pursue and which merits further study.

Summary of conclusions

4.22 From the work we have been able to do so far and bearing in mind current resource constraints we conclude that:

i   in the long term few districts are likely to need more than 150 or so NHS mental handicap beds in all (4.13)

ii   health authorities contemplating new buildings for the mentally handicapped over the next few years should "think small" (4.18)

iii   Before deciding on capital investment in an existing facility both health and local authorities need to consider carefully whether it would be preferable to cater for the clients in adapted or new units off the hospital site (4.18)

4.23   We consider that further thought needs to be given to:

i   the optimum range of sizes for units of different kinds (4.17)

ii   the pattern of services in each locality (4.17)

iii   whether urban and rural areas may require different patterns of service (4.21).

Chapter 5   Staffing

5.1   The quality of any service, wherever it is provided, depends to a large extent on the staff working in it. In this chapter we look at the staffing of the various parts of the services and how this has changed over the years.

TABLE 5.1   WTE Staff in Mental Handicap Hospitals   England

	1969	1977
All Medical Staff	303	450
Consultants in Psychiatry[1]	127	174
Consultants in Paediatrics	2	5
All Nurses[2]	14,536	24,515
Qualified Nurses	8,413	10,702
Other Nurses	6,123	13,813
Domestic Services Staff	N/A	5,795
Managers and Supervisors	N/A	435
Ward Orderlies and Other Domestic Staff	2,554[3]	5,360
Chiropodists	N/A (1970=20)	23
Dentists	17	23
Occupational Therapists		
Qualified	77	113
Helpers, etc	N/A (1970=212 "others")	484
Industrial Work Therapy and Handicrafts Staff		
Qualified	50[4]	78
Others	N/A (1971=317)	406
Physiotherapists		
Qualified	37	103
Helpers, etc	N/A (1970=4 "others")	62
Speech Therapists	18	32
Other Therapists	N/A (1971=285)	269
Psychologists	54	140

[1] Consultants in mental illness, mental illness children and adolescents and mental handicap
[2] 1969 figures for nurses relate to nurses working in the hospital, 1977 to the total nursing staff of the hospital or unit
[3] Not known whether managers, supervisors and other domestic staff included.
[4] Industrial Instructors only.

Hospital Staff

5.2   Table 5.1 gives information about the staffing of mental handicap hospitals (whole-time equivalents). Obviously it does not include all groups of staff but it covers those most closely concerned with providing a direct service to residents. When looking at the table it is worth remembering that over this period the number of mentally handicapped people in hospital declined from 56,300 in 1969 to 47,900 in 1977, but that improved conditions of service for staff may have reduced the hours worked by staff. The figures also conceal substantial regional variations.

5.3   The importance of the nursing contribution is clear. Of the direct care staff included in the table, three-quarters are nurses. Professionals other than nurses are very few and far between. For example there is one speech therapist for every 1,500 hospital residents, one qualified physiotherapist for every 470 and one qualified occupational therapist for every 420. There is one consultant in psychiatry for every 280 residents.

5.4   Nonetheless there have been considerable improvements since 1969. For example, in that year there was one speech therapist for every 3,130 residents, one qualified physiotherapist for every 1,520, one qualified occupational therapist for every 730 and one consultant psychiatrist for every 440. The greatest improvements in staff: resident ratios have been in physiotherapists and psychologists.

5.5   Whilst there has been an improvement since 1969 in the level of domestic staffing, this has been associated with a considerable decrease in the number of residents engaged in domestic taks. The increase in staffing has probably not led, therefore, to a commensurate improvement in domestic standards.

Nurses

5.6   The nurse: resident ratio for 1977 was double that for 1969 though changes in conditions of service mean that more staff are now required in order to provide the same level of service to residents who are probably relatively more dependent than in 1969. But examining this doubling (from 1:4 to 1:2) more closely reveals that the increase has been largely among unqualified staff. Their numbers more than doubled over the period in question, whilst the number of qualified nurses went up by just over a quarter. The proportion of nurses who were qualified fell from 58% in 1969 to 44% in 1977. Furthermore, the recent OPCS Survey found that a quarter of the qualified nurses were qualified only in branches of nursing other than mental subnormality. Of the enrolled nurses who were qualified in subnormality nursing, half had been enrolled by experience, an option open to staff who worked as nursing assistants with the mentally handicapped, full-time, for at least 2 years prior to 1968 because of the opening of the Roll for staff in this field. By no means all nurse tutors working in this field are qualified in mental subnormality nursing.

5.7   It is difficult at present to make any estimates about future trends in the recruitment and training of nurses. At the time of writing consideration is being given to the Jay Committee's recommendation that all staff involved in the residential care of mentally handicapped people, whether in hospital or in local authority homes, should in future receive training under the auspices of the Central Council for Education and Training in Social Work (CCETSW). Whatever the decision on the Jay Report*, staff who have received training in nursing will continue to have a key role. The most recent recruitment figures show a fall in the number of new students and a very small rise in the number of new pupils, with higher wastage of both students and pupils.

*The government has now indicated that whilst accepting the principles underlying this recommendation they believed it would not be right to urge immediate fundamantal changes to present training arrangements. CCETSW and the General Nursing Councils have been asked to establish a Working Group to look at ways of introducing common elements within the separate forms of training.

5.8   In chapter 2 we have referred to mental handicap nurses working in the community. Other nurses working in the community also provide services to mentally handicapped people and their families, and the increasing number of such nurses (health visitors, for example, increased from 7622 in 1971 to 8443 in 1977), should mean that additional help is now available from this source. Such help not only relieves the pressures on scarce specialist staff, but also helps to stress how much mentally handicapped children have in common with other children.

Consultant Psychiatrists
5.9   The picture is a little clearer on trends in the recruitment of consultant psychiatrists to mental handicap hospitals. The number of applicants for each post advertised is low. The proportion of consultants aged 55 or over has remained constant at 35% since 1974/5, but if these consultants retire at an average of 10 a year over the next 5 years, only half the number of posts left vacant by them are likely to be filled by doctors who were previously senior registrars.

5.10   Out of 42 consultant appointments over the last 3 years, half the apointees were previously consultants or locum consultants elsewhere. This suggests that doctors are transferring to mental handicap fairly late in their medical careers. In order to maintain the present number of consultants, it will be essential for doctors to continue to transfer to the specialty from elsewhere.

5.11   The role of the consultant in mental handicap has of course been changing over the years and no doubt it will continue to do so in the future. Doctors have had to grapple with the problem of reconciling their distinctive clinical responsibility with the need to work as part of a team in which other professions also have their own distinct contributions to make. Increasingly, consultants in mental handicap see their work as providing a psychiatric service to mentally handicapped people in a locality, rather than confining their attention to more generalised medical work in a mental handicap hospital.

5.12 The Royal Commission on the National Health Service considered that, while there was a place for the full-time wholly committed specilist in mental handicap, there was much greater scope for appointments which covered 2 psychiatric specialties such as general psychiatry and mental handicap or child psychiatry and mental handicap and this sort of development is supported by the Royal College of Psychiatrists.

Psychologists

5.13 The rapid growth in the number of psychologists working in mental handicap hospitals means that there are now nearly as many psychologists as there are consultant psychiatrists working there. The Trethowan Report on "The Role of Psychologists in the Health Service" suggested that the greatest unmet needs lay in the fields of child psychiatry and mental handicap and that new patterns of care for the mentally handicapped could involve a greatly increased need for psychologists and a change in the orientation of psychological services towards work in a community setting. There seems little doubt that demand for psychologists in the mental handicap services will for some time yet continue to outstrip supply.

Local Authority Staff

5.14 On the local authority side, a common criticism is that many of the staff in homes and day centres are unqualified. We have already seen that this could be said also about many of the direct care staff in hospitals (54% of nurses in 1977). The following tables give information for 1977 about the number of whole-time staff in various forms of local authority provision and their qualifications.

TABLE 5.2 Whole-time Staff of Local Authority Homes for Mentally Handicapped Children   England

Position	Total Whole-Time Staff	Certificate in Residential Social Work	Nursing Qualification	None
Officer in Charge	108	27	32	49(45%)
Deputy Officer in Charge	104	18	20	66(63%)
Other Care Staff	500	22	38	440(88%)
Total	712	67	90	555(78%)

TABLE 5.3 Whole-time Staff of Local Authority Homes for Mentally Handicapped Adults*   England

Position	Total Whole-Time Staff	Certificate in Residential Social Work	Nursing Qualification	None
Officer in Charge	362	49	135	178(49%)
Deputy Officer in Charge	352	20	88	244(69%)
Other Care Staff	481	18	73	390(81%)
Total	1,195	87	296	812(68%)

TABLE 5.4   Whole-time Staff of Adult Training Centres   England

	Total Whole-Time Staff	Dip TCTMH and/or Management Diploma TCTMH	Declaration of Recognition of Experience of TCTMH	None	Unknown
Manager	443	351	8	84(19%)	0
Instructor	3,026	1,029	23	1,980(65%)	3
Other Care Staff	325	145	7	173(53%)	
Total	3,794	1,516	38	2,237(59%)	

Includes staff of the very few homes with places for both adults and children.

5.15   These tables do indeed show that large numbers of local authority staff, particularly those working in residential care, are unqualified. And the figures would be much worse were it not for the numbers of nurses working in local authority homes. 13% of care staff in homes for children and 25% in homes for adults are nurses.

5.16   If we consider the number of whole-time staff per available place, then homes for children come out best with an overall ratio of 1:2.3 and a ratio of qualified staff to available places of 1:10.3. For homes for adults the comparable figures are 1:6.3 and 1:19.8 and for adult training centres 1:10.2 and 1:24.9.

5.17   In addition to residential and day care staff, field social workers make a significant contribution to the welfare of mentally handicapped people and their families. The overall number of field social workers has grown very substantially from 15,100 in 1972 to 24,600 in 1977 and, whilst authorities' practices vary, at least in some places part of this increase has gone towards improving services for mentally handicapped people. Similar considerations apply to the home help service.

Tentative Conclusions

5.18   We must warn against any attempt to draw conclusions from comparisons between hospital and local authority staff. The figures are simply not comparable, nor are the situations to which they apply.

5.19   However it looks as though, for the foreseeable future, mentally handicapped people, both in hospital and in residential homes are going to be cared for largely by unqualified staff. In local authority homes even senior staff may not be qualified. Training which leads to a qualification should be so organised that the maximum number of staff who wish to qualify can do so without too much disturbance to their own family life; there will also be a major role for in-service training for staff, qualified and unqualified, so that they can develop their skills and thus deliver a better service. This will need to be organised sufficiently flexibly to enable all unqualified staff to receive instruction. There will also be an important role for management at all levels to ensure that staff are organised and deployed in the most effective way and that staff are actually putting into effect the skills they have learnt. This will mean ensuring that, as far as possible, each client has an individual training programme, that staff are aware both of the goals to be aimed for with each client and of the general intentions of the care and/or training being provided, and also monitoring that staff actually are working actively with clients.

5.20   Though ratios of nursing staff to hospital residents have doubled over a fairly short period, the Jay Committee called for them to be doubled again, and a number of commentators have suggested that even this was aiming too low. The Jay Committee also called for an improvement in staffing ratios in local authority residential homes. The National Development Group has suggested increasing the number of staff in Adult Training Centres. The Development Team has drawn attention to staff shortages in many of the services it has visited. Yet there is still very little objective evidence on the basis for establishing minimum or optimum staffing ratios. Any single figure is clearly inappropriate, given the variations in need between different clients and at different times of day and night, and the influence of other variables such as the mix between staff of different disciplines and levels of qualification. We have not considered these problems in any detail but further work on them, including possibly some research, might be justified.

5.21   It seems to us unlikely that staff ratios will improve dramatically in the near future and while staff remain insufficient in number in many places, consideration must focus on how best to compensate for shortfalls. We have noted with interest that some research is being carried out into ways of providing care with limited staff numbers in both residential and day settings. Further research into how progress can be made despite limited resources seems to us of very high priority in present circumstances.

5.22   We also believe that it might be fruitful for considerations to be given to setting priorities for the attention of those staff who are available. These might include developing skills whose lack is seriously damaging to clients and for whose acquisition well-tried techniques exist, such as the promotion of continence, or devoting more attention to young people than to those who are older, as the effects of neglecting the young are likely to be felt for longer.

5.23   The scarcity of staff with certain skills of great importance to mentally handicapped people, eg speech therapists, will take years to remedy. We have as yet no idea what sort of staff:resident ratio we should be aiming for, and this is something which merits further consideration. It would be necessary to identify which services require the participation of a trained therapist, which could be carried out by others under the guidance of a trained therapist, and which can be carried out by other staff following some fairly basic training.

5.24   Many members of these scarce professions would not find working full-time with the mentally handicapped attractive. Consideration needs to be given to ways of attracting such people. For example, therapists whose main interest lies in other spheres may be prepared to work with the mentally handicapped on a sessional basis. We accept that there is a general shortage of therapists, but it is only right that the mentally handicapped should have a fair share of the time of those who are available.

5.25   Meanwhile it is important that the skills of those who are available should be effectively deployed where they can be of the greatest value. Scarce staff should not confine themselves to providing direct treatment for a necessarily limited number of clients but should, as far as possible, devise and communicate programmes which can be carried out by aides and others, and participate in in-service training.

Summary of Conclusions
5.26   In the light of the current and likely future staffing situation we conclude that:

i   there will be a major role for in-service training for both qualified and unqualified staff (5.19)

ii   management will have to ensure that staff are organised and deployed in the most effective way and that staff are actually putting into effect the skills they have learnt (5.19)

iii   where it is not possible to recruit a full-time member of staff in a particular discipline, consideration should be given to the possibility of sessions being provided by staff whose main work lies elsewhere (5.24)

iv   scarce staff should not confine themselves to providing direct treatment for a limited number of clients but should devise and communicate programmes which can be carried out by aides and others and participate in in-service training (5.25).

5.27   We consider that further thought needs to be given to whether it is possible and desirable to set priorities for the attention of those staff who are available. (5.22)

5.28   We have not considered the problem of setting minimum or optimum staffing ratios because of the variations in need between different clients in different settings and at different times, but some work on this subject might be useful (5.20 and 5.22). We would also encourage further research on ways of making the best use of existing staff (5.21 and 5.23).

Chapter 6   Finance and Costs

6.1   So far we have looked at developments in the provision of mental handicap services and in the staffing of those services. In this section we look at the overall amount authorities have been spending on services for the mentally handicapped, and at changes in unit costs — the cost of providing a particular service to an individual mentally handicapped person.

Expenditure
6.2   Certain restrictions on expenditure analysis should first be noted. By no means all the expenditure on health and personal social services (HPSS) for the mentally handicapped can be identified from the financial data available nationally. Expenditure on services specifically for the mentally handicapped can be derived for hospital residents and out-patients, and for local authority funded residential places and day care. But expenditure within the Family Practitioner Services, Community Health Services and certain Personal Social Services (eg social workers), though clearly contributing to the total resources devoted to mental handicap services, cannot be apportioned by central analysis. Moreover, comparisons of identifiable expenditure need to be in constant price terms, ie, adjusted to take account of inflation, and this presents technical difficulties which mean that too much cannot be read into changes between one year and the next. And finally, the national accounts for the NHS changed on reorganisation so that comparisons with pre-1974 are difficult though a special exercise was undertaken for 1970. Expenditure on local authority residential and day care services for the mentally handicapped was not separately identifiable in the national returns until 1972/73. Nevertheless the financial analysis does not present a useful broad picture of recent years.

6.3   Between 1974/75 and 1977/78 (the latest year for which figures are available) the identifiable mental handicap share of expenditure on Health and Personal Social Services remained virtually static; in these two years the shares were 4.5% and 4.3% respectively. However these figures conceal important differences between health and personal social services, and between capital and revenue. Table 6.1 shows that:

   a.   for revenue expenditure, the mental handicap programme share of hospital and community health services grew in times of expansion of the health programme as a whole but the more constrained growth of NHS expenditure since 1974-75 has been accompanied by a virtual standstill in the resources devoted to mental handicap; however, during this latter period the mental handicap share of personal social services current expenditure has risen appreciably;

b. capital expenditure on mental handicap has fallen in real terms, both in hospital and community health services and personal social services but the share of capital expenditure going on these services has increased.

TABLE 6.1   All figures are England, £ Million, Survey 78 prices[1] and exclude Joint Finance

NHS Hospital and Community Health Services

Net Revenue Expenditure (Excluding Joint Finance)

	1970–71	1974–75	1977–78	Average Annual Growth Rate
Mental Handicap	153	200	202	4%
Total HCHS	3,095	3,683	3,878	3.3%
% MH	4.9	5.4	5.2	

Capital Expenditure (Excluding Joint Finance)

Mental Handicap	20	14	14	
Total HCHS	394	431	328	
% MH	5.1	3.2	4.3	

PERSONAL SOCIAL SERVICES

Local Authority Net Revenue Expenditure[2] (Excluding Joint Finance)

	1972–73	1974–75	1977–78	Average Annual Growth Rate
Residential homes for the mentally handicapped				
— adults	7.7	11.3	17.8	18.2
— children	3.2	5.2	8.3	21.0
Adult Training Centres	23.3	28.5	33.9	7.8
MH Sub Total	34.2	45.0	60.0	11.9
Total PSS	623.1	811.7	931.6	8.4
Programme Share	5.5%	5.5%	6.4%	

[1] Broadly price levels as at November 1977; for further explanation see "The Government's Expenditure Plans" Cmd 7439 HMSO January 1979.

[2] excluding LA debt charges and revenue contributions to capital expenditure.

Local Authority Capital Expenditure

	1972–73	1974–75	1977–78
Residential homes for the mentally handicapped			
— adults	7.1	10.6	3.6
— children	1.8	3.0	1.0
Adult Training Centres	10.1	10.1	5.0
MH Sub Total	19.0	23.7	9.6
Total PSS Capital Expenditure	125.2	141.3	50.3
Programme Share	15.2%	16.8%	19.1%

6.4   Figures for Joint Finance have been omitted from earlier tables since this source of finance deserves special and separate discussion. Joint financing was introduced in 1976 to assist joint planning between health and local authorities. Its main purpose is to enable health authorities to give financial support to selected local authority social services projects which serve the interests of the NHS as well as the local authority and which can make a better contribution in terms of total care than would be possible if the money were directly applied to NHS provision.

6.5   Allocations to and spending on joint finance in recent years are shown in Table 6.2.

TABLE 6.2   Joint Finance

£million (out-turn or estimated out-turn prices)

	Allocation	Spending
1976–77	8	$4\frac{1}{4}$
1977–78	21	$17\frac{1}{2}$
1978–79	$34\frac{1}{2}$	31
1979–80	$41\frac{1}{2}$	Not available

6.6   Table 6.3 shows the proportion of the total NHS contribution to joint finance funds which local authorities estimate to have received, or expect to receive, from health authorities for spending on mental handicap services.

TABLE 6.3   Proportion of NHS Joint Finance allocated to Mental Handicap

	Capital %	Revenue %	Total %
1976–77	31	8	39
1977–78	18	11	29
1978–79	18	12	30

Thus in 1977–78, over £5 million of NHS money, which might otherwise have been used for hospital services for the mentally handicapped, went on PSS provision.

6.7   Table 6.4 shows how the 1977–78 figures in Table 6.1 change if allowance is made for Joint Finance.

TABLE 6.4   LA Net Revenue Expenditure   £million Survey 1978 prices

	Excluding JF	Including JF
MH Sub-Total	60	60.8
Total PSS	931.6	940.2
Programme Share	6.4%	6.5%
LA Capital Expenditure		
MH Sub-Total	9.6	14.0
Total PSS	50.3	60.6
Programme Share	19.1%	23.1%

It is noteworthy that in 1977–78, almost one-third of total capital spending on Personal Social Services for the mentally handicapped came from Joint Financing.

Unit Costs

6.8   Expenditure data alone do not provide a complete picture; the figures need to be linked to the places available so as to see what has happened to unit costs.

6.9   The average *cost per inpatient day* in mental handicap hospitals in 1977–78 was £11.70, an increase of 50% in real terms over 1970–71. This represents an average increase of over 6% per year, greater than in any other type of hospital (eg in acute hospitals of over 100 beds unit costs went up on average by about 4% per year over the same period though from a much higher base). However, the major part of the increase took place before 1974–75, when unit costs rose on average by 10.5% per year; between 1973–74 and 1977–78 the average annual increase reduced to 3%.

6.10   It is instructive to see what elements go to make up unit cost. The following table shows for 1976 how the daily unit cost was divided between the various services.

TABLE 6.6   Cost per Inpatient Day in Mental Handicap Hospitals   England

	Out-turn prices 1976–77	
	£	£
Patient Care Services		
Nursing Staff	4.6	45
Medical and para medical supporting services	0.3	3
Other medical and dental services and supplies	0.4	3

	Out-turn prices 1976–77	
General Services	£	£
Administation	0.4	4
Catering	1.2	12
Domestic/Cleaning Services	0.9	9
Laundry/linen services	0.5	2
Other general services	2.1	20
(discrepancy in total due to rounding)		

The total cost is almost equally divided between patient care services and general services. The extent of the nursing contribution is again apparent.

6.11 As always, average unit costs conceal wide variations between individual hospitals. All sorts of factors can affect unit costs including differences in occupancy rates, the age and dependency of the residents, variations in local cost conditions and differences in the quality of care. It is therefore very difficult to sort out the impacts of all these variables. It is also difficult to assess from national costings exactly what improvement in the service is being achieved. The Department has commissioned a research project by York University which is making a detailed investigation of costs and changes in service provision in a sample of about 120 mental handicap hospitals.

6.12 The Department's figures for expenditure and activities can be combined to provide an estimate of unit costs of *local authority services* for the mentally handicapped. The latest available refer to the financial year 1977–78 when unit costs in England were estimated as follows (Survey 1978 prices).

	Net Cost	Gross Cost	
residential homes — adults:	£1,473	£2,218	per resident year
residential homes — children:	£5,395	£5,465	per resident year
ATCs		£856	per available place per year.

(These unit costs, which relate to local authorities' own homes, do not include the capital charges which local authorities incur in borrowing funds for capital projects). The gross cost is the total cost including income from sales and from fees and charges: this represents the real resource cost of providing the service, not the cost to the local authority for whom the income is a source of finance. The share of total costs financed from charges is greater in homes for adults than in homes for children (25% as against 1% in 1977–78), and so the net cost differential between the two is considerable. Occupancy rates are somewhat lower in children's homes than in homes for adults (79% as against 87% in 1977–78), and this may account for some of the remaining difference, but the main explanatory factor is likely to be that staffing ratios are generally higher in children's homes.

6.13   Consistent information on unit costs for local authority services is only available from 1972–73 onwards. Up to 1977–78, gross unit costs increased on average each year in real terms by 15% in residential homes for children, 2.7% in residential homes for adults and 0.2% in adult training centres.

6.14   Obviously it is tempting to compare the cost of hospital care with that of services provided by local authorities. Unfortunately, cost comparisons of this kind are far from straightforward. Firstly, like is not being compared with like. For example, hospitals provide not only residential care but a range of supporting medical and training services which are not included in the cost of local authority care and there is no hospital parallel to local authority debt charges. Secondly, there are differences in the age and dependency of residents between hospitals and homes funded by local authorities. Thirdly, there is the question of whose costs are to be considered. For example, local authority costs are reduced by charges but these have to be paid for by the individual resident who will very often have social security benefits as his sole source of income. So there is a hidden cost to the social security scheme. Similarly, isolated hospitals impose high travelling costs on relatives and friends wishing to visit. Fourthly, costs need to be associated with the benefits they are providing — the quality of the care.

6.15   It also has to be remembered that, in a shift from hospital to local authority care, marginal costs rather than average costs have to be considered. For example, the costs saved by discharging one resident from hospital will almost certainly be less than the cost saved per head of discharging 20 residents if this means an entire ward can be closed. This is simply another aspect of the cost of transition, which has to take account of some temporary degree of under-occupancy, and of capital expenditure on buidlings with a short life. Given these uncertanties, we think it unwise in the present state of knowledge to draw any general conclusions. For what it is worth, in 1977–78 the annual cost of hospital care was £4,235, (it is not possible to split the cost between children and adults) that of a local authority residential home for adults £2,218 (gross cost). If the local authority cost is increased by the annual cost of an adult training centre place the local authority total becomes £3,068. Further allowance would need to be made for medical, dental and other supporting services typically provided in hospital. However, true cost comparisons require a body of detailed costing case-studies, based on individual projects and developments and making allowance for the various factors cited.

Tentative Conclusions
6.16   The figures in this chapter need to be viewed against a general background of public expenditure constraints. The rate of growth in expenditure on health and personal social services reduced from an annual average of well over 4% between 1970–71 and 1974–75 to under 2% between 1974–75 and 1977–78. Capital expenditure reduced significantly as part of the health and personal social services contribution to the required reductions in

public spending, the aim being to maintain revenue spending and direct services to patients as far as possible; the rate of increase in growth on current expenditure slowed down. Moreover in 1976–77 the Government tightened up the control of public expenditure by introducing a system of cash limits, whereby the cash required to provide for pay and price changes was estimated at the start of a financial year and no change in the cash limit was made if that estimate was wrong; previously the amount required by such changes had been automatically made available during the year. A cash limit in itself may lead to underspending, but health authorities have a good record of coming close to the cash limit. However, where forecasts of inflation prove low (as in 1976–77) health authorities had to pay more for goods and services than they envisaged so less was available for development. Local authorities faced a similar squeeze though, as fund-raising authorities, they had some recourse elsewhere.

6.17   The financial data for health services suggest that the constraints since 1974, together with demographic pressures and the need to rationalise acute services in order to release revenue for development, meant that health authorities could do little to sustain the previous increase in expenditure on mental handicap services other than their increasing contribution through Joint Finance. The falling numbers of mental handicap patients did increase the resources available per patient and this would permit some improvement in conditions. But the scope for developing local services was restricted by the level of the capital programme. The Government has said that it will maintain the spending plans on the health service up to 1982–83 set out in Cmnd 7439, and these provided for some growth in current expenditure on mental handicap services, though capital expenditure is virtually static. Some information on how far health authorities think they can progress will be available from Regional Strategic Plans; these were based on 10 year resource assumptions of about 1.4% annual growth in current expenditure with capital expenditure holding level, not far removed from the Cmnd 7439 plans.

6.18   Viewed nationally, local authorities have clearly given high priority to the development of mental handicap services — an increasing share of both revenue and capital expenditure has gone to mental handicap though absolute levels of capital expenditure have of course fallen. It remains to be seen whether they can continue to do so given the current economic problems facing the country and the reductions in planned expenditure on local authority services which the Government expects from 1979–80 onwards. The ability of local authorities to support voluntary and private provision may also be affected. It must therefore be questioned whether, at least in the medium term, community care services can develop at the rate needed to permit changes in the hospital service. If not, the pace of discharge from hospital may slow down. There might also be forced expenditure on outdated stock and a continuing need for large hospitals for longer than had been expected.

6.19   In these circumstances it seems to us that careful consideration should be given to how limited resources can best be deployed. We have already referred in Chapter 4 to the need for health authorities to consider carefully how best to use the limited capital resources available. But a broader look seems required, including consideration of the relative contribution of health and social services and the part voluntary effort and voluntary and private services can be expected to play (we discuss this last point in Chapter 9).

6.20   The picture painted in this chapter inevitably poses the question whether expenditure for particular purposes might be identified in planning and earmarked in allocations. However, earmarked funding would be contrary to current Government policy generally on leaving priorities for use of resources at local level and, as regards local authorities, contrary to the principle of the unhypothecated Rate Support Grant. It is here relevant to add that the contribution of joint finance has clearly been an important one particularly on the capital side. The rules governing joint finance have been relaxed in that the Secretary of State will in future consider extending or reviewing agreements on the period of revenue support for jointly financed projects. Nevertheless joint finance in its present form is not by itself enough to bring about a major switch in the balance between health and social services for mentally handicapped people.

6.21   If it were concluded that, even with such aids to more efficient planning and use of resources as might be devised within current Government policy generally, the timetable for achieving White Paper policies, (let alone any further shift to care in the community), is likely to be a very long one, it would seem necessary to consider whether current strategy needed to be modified to bring it into line with public expenditure expectations and, if so, in what way.

Summary of Conclusions

6.22   Present uncertainty about the availability of resources inevitably dominates thinking about future policy on services for the mentally handicapped. We believe that further thought should be given to how limited resources can best be deployed, including consideration of the relative contribution of health and social services and the part voluntary effort and the voluntary and private sectors can be expected to play (6.19).

6.23   Specific suggestions have been made for changing the basis of financing mental handicap services

earmarking central funds.

direct transfer of funds from health to local authorities.

further development of the joint finance approach.

We have not as yet examined the feasibility of these options or the extent to which they could contribute to a more cost-effective management of the services (6.20).

6.24   If the timetable for achieving even White Paper policies appears a very long one, current strategy may need to be revised to bring it into line with public expenditure expectations (6.21).

Chapter 7 Management and Monitoring

7.1   In this chapter we look at some of the problems faced by those whose task it is to manage and monitor services for mentally handicapped people. We shall be less concerned here with the sort of matters which we have discussed in previous chapters, such as numbers of places and the amount of money spent on services. Progress there can be more or less easily summed up in figures. Here we shall be more concerned with the quality of care, and how this can be assessed and monitored. This is an area where information on local authority services is not readily available in the specialist context of mental handicap services. As a result, although we have taken account of such information as we had about the quality of local authority, private and voluntary services, the emphasis of this chapter is inevitably on the NHS.

Factors affecting the quality of care
7.2   There are many intangibles here and it is very difficult to get an overall view from the centre of the quality of mental handicap services up and down the country and how it is changing over time. For one thing, so many factors affect the quality of services. These range from the physical conditions of buildings to such things as management and staff attitudes to the services. It seldom happens that any factor in isolation causes the quality of care to be poor. More often it is the build-up or combination of a series of problems which leads to low standards.

7.3   Poor physical conditions of the buildings and furnishings are often blamed for the low standards of care which have been found in some mental handicap hospitals. Inquiry reports have highlighted this as a problem and attributed to it part of the low staff morale which they encountered. But the physical environment is not universally accepted as a cause in itself. As the Development Team for the Mentally Handicapped point out in their first report: "It has not always been our experience that poor physical conditions are necessarily associated with poor services. In some hospitals we have been pleasantly surprised at the achievements of staff working in the most appalling buildings and cramped conditions without even adequate facilities for washing, bathing or storage of clothing". In a later paragraph, they comment:

> "We have also witnessed in other comparatively modern buildings many of the worst features of institutionalisation; the decor is drab, essentially clinical and unstimulating, with no signs of personal possessions being encouraged and, in the case of some children's

hospitals, little evidence of facilities for play and an absence of toys. It is clear, therefore, that the physical conditions alone cannot bring about an atmosphere without the right approach by the staff concerned".

7.4   There can be no doubt that staff have a strong influence on the material and emotional life of the clients, and therefore on the quality of service. Both inquiry reports and research evidence indicate that the staff's attitude to their work, their degree of commitment and the level of morale are of prime importance. Features which have been identified as significant for high standards of care in a number of studies include a high degree of delegation of decision-making power to staff in charge of homes or units, good communications between staff and a positive attitude on the part of staff to clients' potential.

Management at authority level
7.5   Inquiries into mental handicap hospitals and homes have often blamed deficiencies in management at all levels for the problems which have led to the inquiries being set up. In recent years some such failings have been attributed to the effects of NHS and local authority re-organisation, including a proliferation of levels of management and changes in designation of nursing and administrative officers in hospital units. Even when a hospital is managed locally, there can be a lack of a feeling of responsibility for the management of the service as a whole which in turn can lead to inaction even when problems have been perceived.

7.6   Such problems are not confined to mental handicap hospitals. Some of them, such as the apparent remoteness of some NHS management, apply to other parts of the health service. The consultative paper on the structure and management of the NHS ("Patients First") made proposals which should lead to simpler and more effective management arrangements and to authorities whose members are more closely in touch with those who provide services.

7.7   But the health service has no monopoly of problems — though the failings of the NHS often get the most publicity. Officers in charge of local authority establishments too can often feel out of touch with social services management at head office. Lines of accountability and responsibility may be unclear. Those concerned with a service which does not fall neatly into classic patterns of domiciliary or residential social work, such as adult training centre managers, may feel that there is nobody in social services management who really understands their particular needs and difficulties and is able to offer advice when needed.

7.8   One of the Development Team's main criticisms of local authority services is the lack of co-ordination within social services departments. This insularity results in their failing to obtain the full range of available services for their clients. The Team sees one of the reasons for this as being a lack of direction and back up from senior management, and a generally poor knowledge of management procedures. Local authority managers can be slow in identifying their staff's training needs, in liaising with other agencies and keeping abreast of developments in the care of their clients. The Team found this far more of a problem with social services staff than in the NHS.

7.9   Both health and social services authorities have difficult in looking at their services as a whole, and in considering the functions of their various posts, and the relationship between them; such difficulties are exacerbated in the case of services, such as those for the mentally handicapped, which are provided in part by health authorities and in part by local social services (and education) authorities, but which need to be looked at as a whole if duplication is to be eliminated and gaps filled.

Management at the level of the unit
7.10   At hospital level in the health service, it would seem that tension and even hostility between medical, nursing and administrative heads within the same tier of management are not uncommon, and a number of reasons have been put forward for this. Occasionally the personality of one or more of the "managers" concerned is sufficient to cause communication difficulties which lead to a badly-run service; frequently the problem stems from the uncertainty about the role of each "manager" within the tier. In the past, the consultant, often known as the medical superintendent, had wide-ranging responsibilities extending well beyond his direct clinical responsibility for his patients. Nowadays, there is an increased recognition of the distinctive roles of nurses, administrators, psychologists and other professionals but often there is no local understanding and agreement on the extent of the responsibility and autonomy of decision of each profession. Increasingly, aspects of hospital life, as well as the management of the hospital as a whole, are the responsibility of multi-disciplinary teams, members of which may be uncertain both of the precise function of the team as a whole and of their role within it. Opportunities for passing the buck have also increased.

7.11   Suggestions for improving the management of hospitals have been made by the National Development Group for the Mentally Handicapped in its report "Helping Mentally Handicapped People in Hospital" and the Working Group on the Organisational and management Problems of Mental Illness Hospitals which considered problems common to mental illness and mental handicap services and concluded that many of its suggestions for improvement could also apply to mental handicap hospitals. The common theme of both reports is the delegation of power and responsibility, including financial responsibility, as far as possible within agreed policy objectives. "Patients First" proposes the maximum delegation of responsibility to hospital level and draws attention to the recommendations of the working group referred to above. Management problems, particularly those arising from the difficulty of multi-disciplinary working at a time when the roles and responsibilities of the various professions are by no means certain, are not capable of quick and easy solution, but clear local guidelines on responsibility and authority can be helpful.

7.12   Responsibility for management and monitoring of quality does not lie with top management alone. More than one committee of inquiry has commented on the failure of some charge nurses to pass on information to or to listen to reports from other nursing staff on their ward, and instances have been noted of failures of communication between staff on different shifts. This has a harmful effect both on the attitudes of the junior nursing staff to their work and on the continuity of resident care. (Nurses, perhaps unfairly, bear the brunt of these criticisms because they are the profession in closest and most frequent contact with residents).

7.13 A further consequent deficiency in management has been remarked on in some areas where line managers have failed to recognise or act upon communications problems at a lower level — whether District, hospital or ward. The inadequate or insensitive handling of complaints from staff and residents is also a cause of unrest and ill-feeling within the service. Every committee of inquiry into mental handicap hospitals since 1969 has expressed considerable anxiety about these problem areas and has called for improved guidance, leadership and communication within each discipline involved. It seems likely that such problems would arise less frequently if all units had an agreed operational policy, known to all staff.

7.14 Whilst good management and good communications are essential for a good service, we do not pretend that they can in themselves solve every problem. One charge nurse wrote recently that he no longer bothered to complain when asked to lend out one of his few staff to a ward whose position was even worse. This was not because he accepted the situation as desirable, but because he knew that management were aware of his problems but could not find the money to solve them. The Development Team has come across adult training centres where, even if staff have the appropriate skills to give proper training, the staffing ratio is so inadequate that the staff are unable to use these skills to any real purpose, and are reduced to unconstructive supervision.

Evidence of improvement

7.15 In spite of serious deficiencies, there is evidence that the quality of care is improving. Even in some hospitals which have been the subjects of inquiries, commendable aspects of care have been found, and improvements following particular HAS and Development Team reports have been noticed by the Development Team on their subsequent visits. Examples include:

i   improvements in staff ratios;

ii   establishment of assessment and training schemes for residents and clients living at home;

iii allocation of beds for short-term, on-demand and emergency care;

iv   establishment of group homes from joint finance;

v   appointment of social workers with special reponsibility for the mentally handicapped;

vi   up-grading of toilets, dormitories and other facilities.

The Team's evidence shows improvements not only in the material life of residents but also in the way services are co-ordinated and managed, and better communications between health service and social services department staff in the provision of these services.

Monitoring

7.16 Earlier this year Regional Health Authorities were asked to review their arrangements for monitoring the quality of service being provided in their long-stay hospitals, and to ensure that these were adequate. In the process of this review they have also taken stock of the monitoring arrangements of their constituent Area Health Authorities.

7.17 Virtually all Regions and Areas have instituted regular visits by authority members and officers to supplement the normal discussions about the management of services at member and officer levels; most Regions have devised means of overseeing the monitoring done by Areas; CHC reports of their visits to long-stay hospitals are usually made available to the managing authorities, and most Areas have devised systems for handling complaints, whether from staff, residents or their families.

7.18 Some Regions are still scrutinising their arrangements with a view to improving them still further, and are considering ideas such as improving liaison between NHS and local authority management and how to bring about effective multi-disciplinary management. The consultative document, "Patients First", suggested experiments with advisory groups of NHS officers who would monitor local NHS services and report direct to Districts, with copies to Regions.

7.19 Individual local authorities develop their own methods of monitoring services. Help is available to them from the Department's Regional Social Work Service. Patterns of such monitoring vary widely with some involving the active participation of elected members whilst some involve only staff in a direct management role and yet others entail the appointment of advisors with monitoring responsibilities.

7.20 As health and social services for mentally handicapped people are really two parts of a single comprehensive service, it would seem appropriate for Joint Consultative Committees to consider how health and local authorities can best jointly monitor the service as a whole, as the quality of the service is dependent not only on its individual parts but on how these work together. Members of both authorities have an important role to play in visiting establishments for which they are responsible and equipping themselves for such visits by ensuring that they know the main points to look out for. The National Development Group for the Mentally Handicapped is at present working on a checklist with the aim of helping authorities to monitor their services. Discussion of a checklist could well provide a starting point for joint working in this area.*

*Expected to be published November 1980

7.21 Very little monitoring of the quality of services is carried out at national level. We refer in the next section to the monitoring of certain national minimum standards for hospitals for the mentally handicapped.

7.22 General problems relating to the monitoring of mental handicap services must be seen in the context of similar problems relating to the monitoring of any service, particularly any service providing long-term care. General issues concerning monitoring are the subject of separate study at national level at present, and this would seem to be the most appropriate forum in which to consider many of the matters discussed in this chapter. However, there is already a separate arrngement for helping authorities to monitor services in the form of the Development Team, and we would not wish to rule out completely the possibility of separate monitoring arrangements for mental handicap services.

National Minimum Standards for Mental Handicap Hospitals
7.23 In a very limited area an attempt has been made to set national minimum standards. As long ago as 1969 DHSS issued advice to health authorities on interim measures to improve hospital services for the mentally handicapped, and set out what were considered to be minimum standards in some amenities and aspects of care. Authorities were later told to aim to achieve these standards by 1975 and were allocated additional resources to help them to do so. These standards are only very crude proxies for some aspects of the quality of care.

7.24 By 1973 there were still large numbers of hospitals which were below one or more of the minimum standards despite the increase in unit costs referred to in the previous chapter. After that date there were significant advances in the numbers reaching the minimum levels, although unit cost increases were negligible. This apparent anomaly may well be explained by authorities needing to make a lot of progress in the early years to get near the minimum standards. After that, small improvements may have sufficed to bring them up to standard, as since 1973 there has been a marked improvement in the number of hospitals reaching the standards set for medical and nursing staff ratios, with only 3 hospitals still failing to reach the target by 1977.[1]

7.25 Similar progress has been achieved in the standards for the amount of floor space allocated per resident, although the number of hospitals falling short of the target is higher — 10 with inadequate night space (compared with 20 in 1973) and 7 with inadequate day space (16 in 1973).[2] With this there has been a fall in the number of hospitals with large dormitories from 20 in 1973 to 6 in 1977.

7.26 According to the minimum standards, each resident should have personal cupboard space and personal clothing. The number of hospitals failing to provide personal cupboard space for each resident fell from 15 in 1973 to 6 in 1977.[2] The pattern for personal clothing is less cheering. The number of hospitals which do not conform to this standard has fluctuated

57

between 11 and 6.[2] We know from the development Team that staff are often disheartened by the destructive effect on personal clothing of laundries more used to flat linen.

[1] Figures quoted in paragraphs 7.24–27 relate to hospitals with 200 beds and over.

[2] These figures relate only to those hospitals where 25% or more residents were below the minimum standard of amenity.

7.27   The most difficult standard to achieve appears to be that for ward orderlies and domestic staff. The standard set was 3.5–6.1 hours per bed per week for these services, but in 1977, 54 hospitals were still below this despite the doubling of staff numbers. The improvement since 1973 has been negligible, and the trend has appeared to be for a gradual worsening of the position.

Tentative conclusions

7.28   The lack of hard evidence on the quality of care will be apparent, as will the fact that such information as there is relates largely to the hospital service. There is little evidence about the quality of local authority services and virtually nothing about the quality of private and voluntary services — though in the personal experience of officers of the Department these last include both some of the most forward-looking and some of the least acceptable provision made.

7.29   The management problems facing authorities are substantial. Although there is advice from various quarters, it is not always consistent and there are continuing major diffiulties arising from uncertainty about the roles of the various professions. A number of studies have suggested that clearly defined, written operational policies can be of great assistance, but drawing up such policies requires a considerable amount of work and special expertise. Management training will need to pay greater attention than it does at present to ways of monitoring the quality of services.

7.30   The difficulties facing authorities attempting to decide what to monitor and how to monitor are also formidable. As already mentioned, the National Development Group for the Mentally Handicapped is at present working on a checklist of indicators of the quality of mental handicap services, which it is hoped may provide an aid to monitoring.* Many authorities have found a visit from the Development Team for the Mentally Handicapped useful in drawing their attention not only to things that need improving but to the aspects of care which authorities ought to be monitoring. The officers of the Department's Regional Social Work Service are available to offer advice to local authorities on individual establishments, the service as a whole, and means of monitoring standards within it.

*See footnote to paragraph 7.20

7.31   The intention behind setting minimum standards was to provide an incentive for change in the hospital service. However, although these standards are 10 years old and reflect only what was considered the minimum then, they are not everywhere met even now. Although the Department has monitored progress, competing demands for limited resources have meant that it has never followed up defaulting authorities with any particular vigour, and the standards have thus not been a particularly effective mechanism for change. They do, however, provide almost the only evidence available to the Department on the quality of services, crude though they may be.

7.32   Consideration needs to be given not only to whether it is feasible to set and enforce minimum standards from the centre, but to whether the detailed information — collection and the element of standardisation implicit in such an exercise can be justified. The existing minimum standards are limited in scope yet compliance with them is often difficult to assess (for example, personalised clothing has not been defined); any attempt to set minimum standards over a wider area would run into even greater difficulties of this kind. It seems to us that the prime responsibility for monitoring must continue to lie with field authorities.

Summary of conclusions
7.33   We conclude that:

i   Monitoring is a subject to which Joint Consultative Committees could usefully devote some attention. (7.20)

ii   Management training will need to pay greater attention than it does at present to ways of monitoring the quality of services. (7.29)

iii   The prime responsibility for monitoring must continue to lie with field authorities. (7.32)

7.34   Further consideration needs to be given to the feasibility and desirability of setting minimum standards centrally. (7.32)

7.35   We consider that broader questions of monitoring, covering as they do a wider field than mental handicap alone, should be considered in that wider context, but that the possibility of separate monitoring arrangements for mental handicap services should not be ruled out. (7.22)

Chapter 8 Planning a New Pattern of Services

8.1   The 1971 White Paper stressed how essential it was for services for the mentally handicapped to be planned jointly by health and local authorities and this remains as true today as it was then.

Co-ordination of local services

8.2   Local services need to be co-ordinated so that each individual mentally handicapped person can benefit from those parts of the service which are most appropriate to his needs. Some of these may be administered by health authorities and others by local authorities, including not only social services but also education and housing. Links also need to be built up with those responsible for providing advice on employment, and with social security offices. Only in this way can the best use be made of available facilities, and individual mentally handicapped people derive the greatest benefit from them.

8.3   Communication between different authorities is not always easy to sustain even at this most basic (though by no means least important) level. In Chapter 2 we referred to devices which can help to overcome problems at this level, including formal arrangements for teamwork in the community and the nomination by mutual agreement among those concerned of a named person or key worker who would be responsible for seeing that the handicapped person and his family received appropriate advice and services, co-ordinating the work of those professionals who will need to be involved as of right and bringing in other professionals as required.

8.4   "Patients First" reaffirmed the importance which the Government attaches to effective collaboration between health and local authorities, and stresses that good working relationships between the new district health authorities and local authorities will become increasingly important as community services develop. Where coterminosity is not possible, "Patients First" recognised that it would clearly be desirable that the boundaries of two or more health authorities should be co-terminous with the boundary of a social services authority, or vice versa.

8.5   Joint planning of mental handicap services is now almost universal though the arrangements are not always formalised in Joint Care Planning Teams. Furthermore, the extent to which health and local authorities are equal partners in planning varies enormously, as does participation by such vital contributors to planning as education authorities, housing authorities and parents of mentally handicapped people.

8.6   Difficulties which arise over joing planning of the kind referred to thus far must in the end be resolved at local level, and the first essential is a reasonable amount of goodwill on all sides.

8.7   We would like to draw attention, however, to 3 areas of difficulty which seem to cause problems for even the best laid local plans. These are transport, planning permission and fire precautions.

8.8   Particular difficulties have occurred in some instances over the provision of transport, to the extent that expensive services are under used because nobody can sort out who should be responsible for transporting clients to them, or because those who are responsible do not have the necessary resources. Responsibility for transport between different parts of the system needs to be settled at the planning stage so that people are not deprived of needed and available services. Appendix H quotes the relevant powers.

8.9   Plannning permission is often required for hospitals, homes and hostels for the mentally handicapped. Allowance for delays resulting from planning inquiries must be built into the process of service planning. In general, the less the premises stand out as being different from neighbouring buildings and the smaller the number of people to be accommodated the more acceptable they will be to neighbours — and the better for the users themselves. The development of modern patterns of services for mentally handicapped people means that they will in future live in many localities which are without facilities at present. Experience has shown that communities can be persuaded to accept and indeed welcome mentally handicapped residents, but there are often initial objections from local residents to be overcome. These objections range from fears about how the residents may behave, usually based on lack of knowledge, to anxiety that the presence of mentally handicapped people in the locality will affect property values. There is no evidence that in the long-term there is any impact on local property values.

8.10   Nobody would dispute the value of sensible fire precautions. But there have been occasions when the internal appearance of buildings which have been planned to be domestic in character, or indeed of ordinary houses which have been adapted for the use of mentally handicapped people, have been drastically transformed by the requirements of local fire officers. Such requirements can also add substantially to the cost of a service. Service planners will need to discuss their plans with fire officers and ensure that the latter are aware of the intention to creat a domestic atmosphere.

Planning for the future
8.11   When joint planning means looking jointly further into the future and balancing the need for mental handicap services against other calls on the

funds of health and local authorities, more serious obstacles can arise. These obstacles may even seem insurmountable when, as in the case of residential services for mentally handicapped people, that future should see a move from a geographically distorted, preponderantly NHS service to a service which is both local and more equally divided between the NHS and local authorities. Such a move would require a general build-up in social services provision and a build-up in NHS provision in many areas, both of which need to be timed to coincide with a run-down of unsuitable NHS facilities concentrated in a relatively small number of areas. In discussion with health authorities the Department has sometimes found that the limited amount of capital available has been seen as a bar to any early development of District services, though an increasing number of authorities are finding that a start can be made in a modest way with a small base and an identifiable team.

8.12   These are not the only difficulties. One major problem is that health and local authorities have completely different concepts of forward planning. Health authorities are required by the DHSS to plan much further ahead than local social services authorities, who in any case are only requested to let the DHSS have an indication of their future spending intentions: this reflects the different relationship between the different types of authority and the Department.

8.13   A second complication is that the methods of financing of the 2 sets of authorities are different. This is something which field authorities themselves see as a difficulty. The health services is funded through money voted by Parliament for that specific purpose and handed down a "chain of command" to authorities which remain ultimately responsible to the Secretary of State. Social services are funded partly through the rates and partly through the rate support grant negotiated annually between central and local government. Although calculation of the rate support grant includes a notional element for social services as for other services provided by local government, local authorities are free to divide the money they receive from rate support grant among their various functions as they please.

8.14   Thirdly, local authorities, being elected bodies, are more likely to be affected by changes in policy depending on which party is in power at any one time. Members of local authorities, being directly answerable to a local electorate, are also more likely than members of health authorities to consider the popularity of their policies with voters. Such considerations can have a potent effect, particularly at local level.

8.15   Fourthly, as mentioned earlier, although on the map most area health authorities have the same boundaries as one or more social services authorities, in a number of cases the area actually administered by the health authority is not the same as the one appearing on the map. Below the level of the authorities themselves the administrative boundaries, for example of health districts and of social services areas are often quite different. The Government's proposals for changes to the structure and management arrangements of the NHS may mean that in future more local authorities will have to plan jointly with more than one health authority.

8.16 These difficulties affect all forms of joint planning. But the problem of moving from the existing pattern of services to one of comprehensive services in each locality is not one that can be resolved at the level of the individual health or local authority however well they work together. For example, those authorities which at present administer large mental handicap hospitals find it quite impossible to plan for the future when they do not know if and when they will be relieved of the responsibility of caring for people at present in those hospitals whose homes were originally in other areas.

8.17 The obvious place to turn when problems are too difficult for Areas and their matching local authorities to solve alone is to Regional Health Authorities. But the problem sometimes spans more than one Region, particularly in the London area. Furthermore, and of far greater significance, Regions have no mechanism for joint planning with local authorities.

8.18 Regional plans should in theory reflect the joint planning which has taken place at Area level and should be included in Area plans, but discussions which the Department has had with Regions on their plans indicate that many Regions have only a very general (and usually pessimistic) idea of local authorities' intentions, even though the realism of Regional intentions can only be judged when matched against those of local authorities. Virtually none have any machinery for a regular and informed exchange of views with local authorities.

Some examples of positive planning

8.19 Nevertheless, despite the daunting problems described, we should like to quote a couple of instances where positive long-term plans are being made.

8.20 An example of planning at Area level is in *Northumberland*, where the Planning Team has proposed a pattern of residential service based on "core" homes linked to small, defined local communities, for which houses will be rented or purchased. These well staffed "core" homes linked to small, defined local communities, for which houses will be rented or purchased. These well staffed "core" homes will provide accommodation for a small group of people including the "most handicapped". In addition, they will provide short stay care for that community together with support to a cluster of alternative residences including the family home, group home, and other staffed homes. This residential service will be set in the context of the wider network of support already developed which includes specialist community nurses, social workers, and psychologists. These ideas draw heavily on work pioneered in Nebraska (ENCOR), which is also the inspiration for new services planned in Cardiff (NIMROD).

8.21 The *Wessex RHA* are continuing their pioneering role in setting up small local hospital units for severely mentally handicapped people. A 10 year programme has been drawn up to provide over 700 places in local units and to restructure and reduce the size of the large hospitals, pending their complete replacement. Wessex intends to work with other agencies to provide an integrated service to mentally handicapped people at home recommending that each family should have a 'key worker' and that the 'Portage' home education scheme for pre-school children should be extended. The health authorities will promote the development of supported housing schemes for the more able mentally handicapped now in hospital. Local hospital units admit 'NHS depndency' people living within the defined catchment area. Units are independently managed, have a domestic style with family groups and houseparents, and intend to cater for the full range of social, and with other agencies, occupational and educational needs. The maximum size is 25 places (of which 4 are for short term or emergency care) but a pilot project is under way to assess the cost and staffing implications of setting up units for 6–8 people. Routine medical, dental and social care are provided by the usual local services with specialised care by visits from the relevant professions or at the District General Hospital. One member of each DMT/ATO/RTO has been designated to act as the focus for implementing and monitoring the policy.

A Single Service

8.22   In Chapter 6 we referred to two possible measures which some people think might ease some of the problems of joint planning (earmarking central funds and the direct transfer of funds from health to local authorities). Others propose more radically, that either the NHS or local authorities should take over complete responsibility for services for mentally handicapped people or even that a separate service should be set up. Admittedly, such solutions might relieve the burden of joint planning but they could create more problems than they solved. For example, new boundaries of responsibility would be created which might well be no more rational than those which exist at present.

8.23   A separate service has the additional disadvantage that it would imply that mentally handicapped people are somehow "different" from the rest of the population, whereas current policy stresses the need for them to be integrated with the community as a whole.

8.24   However, such a service might possibly be seen as an interim measure to enable change to take place more rapidly, as happened in Denmark where services, having been developed as a separate service, are now being handed over to the local authorities.

8.25   Further thought would clearly be required before serious consideration was given to major changes in the responsibilities of health and local authorities or to the possibility of a separate service.

Tentative conclusions

8.26   We believe that co-operation between authorities on ensuring that there is a co-ordinated approach to the problems of each individual mentally handicapped person is properly a matter for local solution and that sufficient guidance and advice on these matters is probably available. We would stress, though, that arrangements for co-operation and co-ordination need to extend beyond health and social services to include education, housing, employment and the views of parents.

8.27   We also believe that joint planning at local level must continue, because it is at that level that detailed decisions about the service to be provided must be made.

8.28   In Chapter 6 we referred to suggestions which have been made for changing the basis of financing mental handicap services. We believe that, whether or not any of these suggestions are considered, further thought needs to be given to ways of tackling some of the planning problems which we have discussed earlier in this chapter. The White Paper objective of providing more services in the community, which must entail a declining role for the large mental handicap hospital, is generally accepted, but the means of achieving this have not been adequately considered.

Summary of Conclusions

8.29   We conclude that:

i   co-operation between authorities on operational planning is properly a matter for local solution (8.26).

ii   joint strategic planning at local level must continue (8.27).

8.30   We consider that further thought must be given to ways of tackling some of the planning problems which stand in the way of the development of local service (8.28).

8.31   We have not looked in any detail at the possibility of making major changes in the responsibilities of health and local authorities or establishing a separate mental handicap service (8.25).

Chapter 9   The Role of the Voluntary and Private Sectors

9.1   This document has concentrated so far on the services provided by the NHS and by local authorities. This is inevitable, as the Department has a fair amount of information about the situation in these services, whereas, as we shall see, information about the voluntary and private sectors is scanty. However, these sectors make an important contribution to the services which are available to mentally handicapped people and, at their best can provide a degree of flexibility which the statutory services can never expect to emulate.

The Range and Scope of Voluntary and Private Provision
9.2   Voluntary and private agencies provide a wide range of services. In the residential field these vary from the invididual landlord with a mentally handicapped tenant, through unstaffed accommodation, small residential units, and nursing homes to private hospitals.

9.3   The quality of services provided varies from truly excellent to, in the case of some unregistered homes, grossly inadequate. At its best voluntary and private provision can offer mentally handicapped people a way of living in the community which is designed to cater for their individual needs and to help them achieve the maximum possible independence. At its worst, unregistered private provision may represent minimal care by inadequate members of unqualified staff in near-slum conditions; and with proprietors who, acting as appointees for residents may divert their social security entitlement for no obvious benefit to the residents. One case which came to light involved mentally handicapped people living in over-crowded conditions with no bed linen or towels, and working for the owner of the house they were living in (who collected their social security benefit) for pocket money.

9.4   Besides residential services provision in the voluntary and private sector includes day services, fostering and adoption schemes and arranging employment opportunities for mentally handicapped people, as in MENCAP's Pathway scheme which provides pre-training for employment and arranges places in industry where the mentally handicapped person concerned is assigned initially to the special care of a "foster worker." Many voluntary bodies have been active in pioneering new forms of service which have later been taken up by the public sector.

9.5   In some respects, voluntary provision goes beyond what is available from the public sector, and this is particularly true in the area of leisure and recreation. Several voluntary organisations arrange leisure activities which are particularly valuable for otherwise isolated mentally handicapped people. MENCAP's Gateway clubs provide activity and leisure clubs for over 16 year olds for example.

9.6   Such activities contribute to the range of local services available, but there is some evidence of a tendency for private residential provision to cater for a national catchment area, with consequential problems in maintaining contact with families and the home community. Voluntary bodies are more likely to have more clearly defined catchment areas for the services they provide.

9.7   Voluntary organisations may also function partly or wholly as pressure group, as fund raising organisations or as self-help groups and we shall look at these activities later in the chapter.

Village Communities

9.8   Village communities are a service which is only provided by the voluntary sector, though in some respects their underlying philosophy is similar to that which gave rise to the setting up of the "colonies" which have now become the large mental handicap hospitals. Unlike the hospitals, though, they frequently owe their origin to the efforts of parents of mentally handicapped people concerned to provide care and support to their offspring throughout life.

9.9   Such communities are most usually situated in rural areas, often with considerable acreage attached, and provide total living and working experience for their members. Mentally handicapped people under the guidance of staff run the farms, look after gardens and care for animals. They are involved in craft and production work, sometimes reaching a very high level of skill.

9.10   On the whole, the residents of the villages are without a substantial degree of physical handicap and are not profoundly intellectually handicapped. Most communities select members who will integrate into the group and therefore have reservations about mentally handicapped people with behaviour disturbances or severe emotional problems. However, over recent years some establishments have accepted some mentally handicapped people with a wider range of difficulties.

9.11   In the past some village communities have been criticised for their isolation from the general population, for their over-protective attitudes, the limited range of educational opportunities offered and their selectivity over residents. The concept is, however, very popular with parents, and many of the communities, aware of the criticism, have over the past few years made considerable efforts to integrate into the wider community and to extend the service they offer, for example, by developing accommodation outside the community.

The Extent of Voluntary and Private Provision

9.12   DHSS statistics about voluntary and private provision and sparse, relate only to residential provision and almost certainly under-estimate the scale, since the main sources are registration data and returns on use of these facilities by local authorities. Mental nursing homes should be registered with health authorities; residential homes with local social services departments. However, some establishments may be registered as non-maintained schools; some may not be registered at all. Some residents in ordinary children's homes or homes for the elderly will be mentally handicapped but appear in a different set of statistics. Most importantly, perhaps, statistics are collected only on places used by mentally handicapped people for whom local authorities are responsible. Bearing these reservations in mind, the following figures should be regarded as a minimum.

9.13   According to the Department's statistical returns approximately one fifth of the 11,200 places available to local authorities in homes and hostels for mentally handicapped adults in 1977 were provided by voluntary organisations and over 5% by private organisations. Similarly voluntary organisations provided 15% and private organisations nearly 5% of the 2,200 places available to local authorities for children. In addition at least 590 adults were living in lodgings arranged and currently supervised by social services departments.

9.14   There are also a number of mentally handicapped people living in private mental nursing homes, resitered under the Nursing Homes Act 1975. Total bed provision is about 3,500 but it is not known how many are for mentally handicapped people as the figures also include beds occupied by those who are mentally ill. At present over 700 mentally handicapped people are accommodated in the private sector under contractual arrangements with the NHS.

Quality Control

9.15   The quality of voluntary and private residential provision should to some extent be controlled by registration requirements (see Chapter 2) which vary according to the legislation under which the home is registrable.

9.16   Voluntary and Private residential homes for mentally handicapped people should be registered with local social services departments under section 37 of the National Assistance Act 1948. Registration requirements contain only a few specific provisions and much is left to the registering authority; discretion in determining what is adequate for each home. There is also doubt as to whether certain types of premises are registrable at all. Authorities vary in the number and thoroughness of inspections and the standards they set.

9.17   Registration arrangements for a whole range of voluntary and private social services provision are at present under review. The general aim is to focus the provisions more clearly and possibly to offer guidance on the general criteria for registration decisions. Changes in the provisions may have significant implications for social services authorities' resources (both financial and in terms of trained and experienced staff). Information has been obtained on their present registration practices with the intention of consulting on options for change during the course of 1980. We mention here some of the problems we see in the mental handicap field.

9.18   There seems to be a marked reluctance on the part of local authorities to register private establishments which purport to be lodging houses or private hotels but whose "guests" are predominantly mentally handicapped or mentally ill. This may well be because in respect of places not providing more than board and lodging the legislation — and more especially the view of the Courts upon it — is uncertain. Reluctance to register may also occur, however, when the consequentials of registration, such as inspection, have resource implications for authorities which they find unacceptable. Some authorities may also feel it preferable to distance themselves from these lodging houses so that they may disclaim responsibility should difficulties arise over standards of care or living conditions.

9.19   Current provisions do not allow for refusal of registration as a residential home on the grounds of an excessive concentration of establishments in a particular locality, though this may be taken into account by planning authorities if planning permission is required. The wish to avoid seeking planning permission may of course be a further disincentive to registration, as registering a "private hotel" as a home for mentally dosordered people might well be considered a change of use. There have been a number of instances where district councils have complained about a concentration of mentally ill and mentally handicapped people in their locality. Seaside towns are particularly susceptible to this, as landladies may see an all year round income as preferable to relying on declining seasonal trade. Some, indeed, have found caring for the mentally handicapped rewarding in more ways than one and private an excellent service. Others provide the bare minimum. It is, however, the concentration of establishments rather than the standard of service which gives rise to local concern.

9.20   A further problem with registration is that it gives establishments a "seal of approval" which, at least as time goes by, they may not merit. Standards, especially in fire precautions, have risen appreciably over the last 10–20 years. Premises registered perhaps 15 years ago met the standards accepted at that time, but may not have matched rising standards since then. Registration is difficult to withdraw both because of the difficulties in establishing a case for doing so and because, if the establishment were forced to close, the local authority might be expected to find alternative places for the residents.

9.21   Organisations operting in more than one local authority area are perplexed by the differing expectations of different local authorities and what is reported to them by the local authorities as the lack of clear Departmental guidance on criteria and standards for registration. Confusion can also arise as to when an establishment should be registered as a nursing home, with the

Department of Education and Science, or even with the Department of Employment.

9.22   The Nursing Homes Act 1975 provides that any premises used for the provision of nursing or other medical treatment (including care and training under medical supervision) for one or more mentally handicapped or mentally ill people should be registered with the area health authority as a mental nursing home. Registration requirements are concerned with the adequacy of standards of nursing care and the accommodation and other facilities provided by such homes, which are required to be inspected by the registering authority at least once every 6 months. The authority has power to interview and examine any resident in private where it is felt they are not receiving proper care.

9.23   It is recognised that there are variations in the assessment of adequacy by registering authorities and in the standards of mental nursing homes. The Health Services Bill currently being considered by Palrliament* includes provisions to clarify the qualifications and level of nursing staff in homes registered under the 1975 Act, aimed at ensuring that the staffing reflects the type and number of patients in a home. Also the regulations governing the conduct and registration of homes are being consolidated and brought up to date. The revised regulations will set out in more detail the type of facilities which homes should provide to an adequate standard. The Department will also be issuing guidance on registration of nursing homes and the monitoring of standards in those homes.

*The Health Services Act 1980 received Royal Assent in August 1980

9.24   In order that co-operation between nursing homes and the NHS may develop, guidance will soon be issued to health authorities relaxing a number of administrative barriers to extending contractual arrangements with the private sector.

Finance

9.25   Provision may be described as "private" or "voluntary" but this does not mean that it is without support from the public purse. Voluntary and private organisations rely on fees and charges which may be met either by a health or local authority or by the resident himself which, in effect, usually means from social security payments; or by a mixture of the two. Most voluntary and private establishments are only enabled to operate by authorities paying the fees of residents they sponsor. Health and social services authorities can either pay fees and charges in respect of individual or may have contractual arrangements whereby they pay for the use of a number of beds in a private establishment.

9.26   In addition health and local authorities can make grants to voluntary organisations providing a local service, and central government can also make grants under various Acts, though the Department of Health and Social Security does not normally use its powers to assist with local schemes nor to fund capital expenditure on building schemes. Health authorities may also use joint funding to finance projects by voluntary organisations where the local authority has sponsored the scheme and represents the voluntary body in any discussion with the health authority in Joint Consultative Committees.

9.27   Sometimes landlords are paid higher than average rents to compensate for accepting tenants who may need more help than most: whether the cost of such enhancement should fall on the SBC or on local authorities is one of the matters being considered in current reviews of the supplementary benefits scheme and of local authority fees and charges.

9.28   Thus, though members of voluntary bodies contribute in cash and in kind to the activities undertaken, and most voluntary bodies also raise funds from the public, much of the finance for the sort of voluntary and private provision discussed thus far comes from public funds.

Other Activities of Voluntary Organisations

9.29   The role of voluntary organisations is not confined to the provision of services. A major concern of some organisations is to act as a pressure group — in other words, to see that the needs of the mentally handicapped receive a full measure of public attention. Such activities are particularly valuable when directed at bringing about specific improvements in services at local level, but they also have a role in educating and informing public opinion, thus helping to ensure that the needs of the mentally handicapped are not neglected when plans for expenditure and services are being drawn up.

9.30   Some voluntary organistions provide courses, including workshops and seminars for staff working with mentally handicapped people, foster parents and voluntary workers. The British Institute of Mental Handicap, for example, arranges a number of courses and workshops which are used by health authorities and social services departments for their staffs. The Spastics Society runs courses at Castle Priory College.

9.31   Most voluntary organisations devote a considerable amount of time and effort to fund raising and for some, such as the Leagues of Friends of hospitals, this is their main purpose, though they also often provide certain amenities for residents. It is recognised that available public funds can never meet all the demands likely to be made on them and that voluntary funds to supplement these resources should be welcomed and encouraged. Clause 4 of the Health Service Bill will for the first time give health authorities the power to initiate and support fund raising activities to supplement their exchequer funds.

Parents

9.32   A particularly valuable form of voluntary activity is the bringing together of parents of mentally handicapped people to provide mutual support based on shared experience. The sharing of problems with people who have been through them themselves can result in the mutual exchange of valuable advice.

9.33   There is also room for a constructive partnership between parents, other volunteers and professional workers in providing practical support to enable families to continue to look after their mentally handicapped relative at home and in enabling parents to participate in training programmes which can help their child towards greater independence. Schemes such as Portage and the Parent Involvement Project at Manchester University aim to develop this sort of partnership. In some places the concept of "shared care" has been developed. Parents are involved in the care of their children, who have been admitted to residential accommodation, so relieving the pressure on care staff and helping parents to feel that they retain some responsibility for the care of their children even though they can no longer look after them all the time.

9.34   As receivers of help and advocates for their mentally handicapped relative families must be closely involved not only in decisions about their own relative but also in the planning of mental handicap services generally. This means not only consultation on proposed developments but also participation in the formulation of plans. Such participation is obviously made easier if representative organisations of parents exist and if they can be supported by access to advice on how to assess the quality of services, such as that given in MENCAP's Stamina documents.

Volunteers

9.35   Voluntary effort is not, of course, confined to voluntary organisations. Individual volunteers can play a useful part in helping bridge the gap between residents in hospitals or hostels and the community and in performing tasks which relieve pressures on staff. The White Paper went into some detail on this subject, and the NDG has given advice on the use of volunteers in "Helping Mentally Handicapped People in Hospital". We wish here only to point to one or two developments since 1971.

9.36   A number of mental handicap hospitals employ a fully salaried Voluntary Services Organiser and the National Development Group has recommended that all hospitals with over 200 beds should do so. The task of either the VSO or other members of staff responsible for the work of volunteers is to encourage voluntary organisations, schools, etc to provide volunteers to work in hospitals and to ensure that the right relationship is established between staff and volunteers and that the most fruitful use is made of the volunteers' time and abilities.

9.37   We know of at least one example of a scheme whereby volunteer students spend a year living in flats which are also occupied, on a permanent basis, by mentally handicapped people. Such a form of personal service may commend itself to others.

9.38   Volunteering is not just a one-way process. Some mentally handicapped people also help others by participating in activities of groups that themselves provide voluntary services to people in the community. Whilst this needs to be organised carefully, it can bring great benefit to mentally handicapped people to find themselves in a position to give to others.

Tentative Conclusions

9.39   There are areas in which voluntary enterprise is undoubtedly best. Self-help groups, for example, provide a form of support no statutory service could supply. Both voluntary and private provision can respond quickly and flexibly to newly identified needs, and in this respect may be superior to statutory agencies. Many imaginative and forward looking schemes have come from voluntary organisations. We believe that further consideration could be given to how self-help groups and pioneering work by voluntary organisations can best be helped to develop.

The popularity of village communities raises the question of whether this concept is also worth examining further both for those for whom they at present cater and for the more severely handicapped.

9.40   Both voluntary and private provision of residential accommodation fulfil a very real need and without such provision mentally handicapped people and the authorities statutorily responsible for helping them would be in very real difficulties. In the past, however such provision has often been developed without consideration of the extent to which similar facilities were already being provided locally in the public sector. To some extent the public sector has also ignored what is available in the way of voluntary and private provision. We consider that further consideration should be given to how partnership between the statutory and private and voluntary sectors can be developed in both the planning and delivery of services so that the total range of services available are used to the best purpose.

9.41   It is desirable that private and voluntary provision should not shrink but should at the very least maintain its position. However, there are two interwoven problems which may mean that voluntary and private provision does not expand as much as might be desired particularly when public expenditure is restrained. These two areas are finance and quality control.

9.42   We have seen that some kinds of voluntary and private provision depend heavily on public money. Health and local authorities may find paying for places in voluntary and private provision cheaper than providing their own, but this will by no means always be true. They will, in any case, wish to ensure that the taxpayer's or ratepayer's money is being well spent, when they pay fees and charges to organisations which are not publicly accountable in the same way as they are. Placing a mentally handicapped person in a voluntary or private establishment may be a long-term commitment by an authority, involving substantial expenditure over the years.

9.43   Value for money must include assessing the quality of care provided and this will include ensuring that developmental and educational needs are being met, particularly where children are concerned. Yet, with manpower resources stretched, checking up on registered establishments and keeping in touch with clients in private or voluntary homes or a lodging may take a back seat. Authorities will therefore have to decide on the merits of each case whether it is preferable to place clients in their own establishments where quality, as well as expenditure, can be monitored and where they can exert a greater influence over the care being given to particular individuals.

9.44   Further thought needs to be given therefore to the scope for breaking through the barriers in these areas. Long-term care is expensive. Few people could afford to pay fees for their relatives, and the health insurance companies have not shown interest in the past in providing insurance in this area.

9.45   One possible topic for consideration might be whether the current balance between health and local authorities and the social security scheme in meeting the cost of individuals using private and voluntary services is right. If more of the cost could be borne by the social security system rather than by health and local authorities then authorities might be happier to encourage voluntary and private provision to expand though it could be borne in mind that local authorities (but not health authorities), do have power to charge residents in their own accommodation and thus, indirectly, to pass some of their own costs on to the social security scheme. Any suggestion that more of the cost should be transferred to the social security scheme would require a considerable amount of thought before it was pursued, and problems related to monitoring quality would remain. Indeed, some of the worst squalor has occurred where residents have been paying their own charges from social security benefits.

9.46   We believe that both to protect the interests of mentally handicapped people and to ensure that public money is well spent, encouragement of the use of private and voluntary provision ought to be accompanied by consideration of ways of ensuring that at least a minimum standard of service is provided. In our view, such consideration ought not to be confined to services for the mentally handicapped. The current review of local authority registration arrangements might perhaps be the most suitable forum in which this consideration might take place. Separate guidance on registration of nursing homes will be forthcoming as a consequence of the Health Services Bill currently being considered by Parliament. We recognise, however, that a wish to ensure proper standards of care in the private and voluntary sectors ought to be accompanied by an equally vigorous effort to ensure proper standards of care in the public sector.

Summary of Conclusions
9.47   We conclude that the voluntary and private sectors, have much to offer mentally handicapped people but that encouragement of the use of voluntary and private provision ought to be accompanied by consideration of ways of ensuring that at least a minimum standard of service is provided. Such consideration can best take place in the context of the current review of social services registration requirements and the proposed guidance on registration of nursing homes (9.46).

9.48   We also believe that further thought should be given to:

   i   how partnership between the statutory and voluntary and private sectors can be developed (9.40)

ii   ways of encouraging a greater use of voluntary and private provision (9.44) including the balance of responsibility for meeting the cost of individuals using such private provision (9.45)

9.49   Other matters which might merit consideration are:

i   how self-help groups and pioneering work by voluntary organisations can best be helped to develop (9.39)

ii   whether there is an unmet need for more village communities for the more severely mentally handicapped and, if so, how the setting up of such communities can be encouraged (9.39).

Chapter 10   Conclusion

10.1   Inevitably, preceding chapters have looked at various aspects of services for the mentally handicapped almost as if there were a number of discrete questions which could be examined and answered independently. These quetions are:

— What services are provided for mentally handicapped people at present, and how do these match up with the aspirations expressed in the mental handicap White Paper? Do these aspirations now require redefinition? (Chapter 2).

— How many mentally handicapped people need services, and what characteristics influence this need? How far should services take account of the special needs of particular groups of mentally handicapped people? (Chapter 3).

— What is the size of facilities for mentally handicapped people, how consistent is this with national guidance and should the latter be altered? (Chapter 4).

— What inputs in terms of staff and money have been supplied to mental handicap services since the White Paper and what are likely future needs and problems? (Chapters 5 and 6).

— What problems and progress have been experienced in the management, monitoring and planning of mental handicap services, and how can future advance be achieved? (Chapters 7 and 8).

— What role is played by the private and voluntary sectors in meeting the needs of mentally handicapped people? (Chapter 9).

10.2   In this concluding chapter, we attempt to draw together the main themes which emerge from out study and, without wishing to repeat or summarise all the conclusions reached in each chapter, to indicate those aspects which seem to us the most significant, particularly as regards the prospects for future development of services for mentally handicapped people.

10.3   One of our problems throughout our stocktaking exercise has been a lack of reliable and consistent information. A great deal is known about mental handicap hospitals, but much of it is difficult to interpret. Less is known about other health services or, in terms which relate separately to mentally handicapped people, about local authority services, and there is virtually no systematic information either about private and voluntary provision or about the extent to which mentally handicapped people make use of services provided for the population generally. More is known about the quantity than about the quality of services provided, and the latter is particularly difficult to measure. There is considerable difficulty in assessing the level of need for services and in relating what we know about need to the types of services that should be provided.

10.4   We would be loath to suggest an increase in the amount of information collected by the Department. We are conscious that at times we have been surprised at the amount of information which is available in the Department if sufficient effort is made to dig it out. In some cases, this is a question of presenting raw data in a way which is different from that used in the published tables of statistics. In others, it means that information is being collected which never gets used except on rare occasions such as a review like this or perhaps when a Parliamentary Question is put down. Some information which is readily available in published form seems to be of little use, though we appreciate that others outside the Department have different information needs.

10.5   A general review of the statistical information collected by the Department is under way. We welcome this and hope it will be possible, by reducing the amount of information collected in some areas, to make room for information to be collected in areas where it is almost totally lacking at present.

The salient facts
10.6   Mentally handicapped people are a small and heterogeneous group needing a multiplicity of services. Our evidence does not support the view held in the past that the best measure of prevalence is crude population. We have seen information about variations in prevalence between different localities and we now believe planners must work on the basis that the number of people requiring provision within the locality for which they are planning might lie anywhere within the range of 2.9 per 1,000 population to 3.4 per 1,000 population.

10.7   Though there has been a considerable expansion of local authority day and residential places for adults, and a corresponding increase in expenditure, the numbers still fall short of what is required to meet assessed need. The number of local authority residential places for children has grown disappointingly slowly. The number of people in mental handicap hospitals has been decreasing gradually, but is still far in excess of what the White Paper suggested would be right — and we suspect that the White Paper set the figure too high, rather than too low. Expenditure on mental handicap hospital services has increased substantially in real terms since the White Paper, but the rate of increase has come to a virtual halt in recent years, relying on reduction in numbers to improve the quality of the services though staffing and amenities still leave much to be desired.

10.8   Although there has been an improvement in services provided specifically for mentally handicapped people living in the community, little is known about how far they have benefited from the expansion which has taken place in services provided for the population as a whole, or about the extent to which the staff of these services are equipped to recognise and meet the needs of mentally handicapped people who will, for most of these staff, be a relative rarity. Yet such services are crucial to the maintenance of mentally handicapped people in the community.

10.9   The geographical distribution of mental handicap services remains strikingly uneven. Most local authorities make at least a minimal degree of provision specifically for the mentally handicapped, though the level varies markedly and is nowhere adequate. By contrast, a few health authorities are caring for enormous numbers of mentally handicapped people, including a fair proportion for whom local authority provision would be more appropriate. Yet over three-eighths of health Districts have no local in-patient provision at all for mentally handicapped people.

10.10   Despite substantial numerical increases since the White Paper in all types of staff employed in mental handicap services, there is considerable evidence that more are needed. There is a particular shortage of qualified staff of all kinds. Research points to the crucial role played by the organisation and deployment of staff, and to the need for collaboration if the skills of all staff are to be used to the best effect. The evidence of inquiries and the observations of the Development Team indicate how much still remains to be achieved in these respects.

Quality of Care

10.11   A recurring theme of this document has been concern about the quality of service being provided. Unlike many consumers of health and social services, many mentally handicapped people are unable to assess for themselves the quality of care they are receiving. Many have nobody to act on their behalf and, even where parents and others might be moved to complain, they may be hesitant to do so, knowing that in many instances the problems are so great that they are beyond the capacity of direct care staff to resolve. Furthermore, there are aspects of the care of the mentally handicapped which are difficult for those without knowledge of the field to assess. For example, key issues in good practice include initial and continuing assessment, the provision of programmes related to individual needs, the importance of clear role definition for staff, with maximum delegation of responsibility and interdisciplinary collaboration, the need for full involvement of families in the services provided for a mentally handicapped relative and the importance of allocating staff to relatively small groups of clients with whom they can establish continuing relationships.

10.12   It might perhaps be felt that concern about the quality of care being provided is a luxury in times of economic restraint. We hope that the following extracts from a recent Development Team report will show that this is not so. We wish to point out that, despite the conditions described, the Team were able to praise the staff on both wards for their caring attitude.

"At the time of team's visit 10 [beds] were occupied. 4 [patients] were epileptic and 2 incontinent ... Furniture was dilapidated but the charge nurse had resuced most of it when it was rejected from other wards. One bedroom was overcrowded, foul smelling and untidy ... The toilet and wash areas were dirty, foul smelling and bare. There were no towels, soap etc. The only store cupboard was off the ward downstairs".

"20 beds ... The majority required assistance with feeding, washing and dressing. 13 were incontinent, 6 were toilet trained, 1 had speech and the other 19 could understand simple instructions ... For night duty there was 1 nursing assistant full time, and 2 part-timers providing 20 hours each ... 18 of the patients remained on the ward all day ... There were no individual training programmes".

10.13 We have pointed out that problems such as these are not confined to the NHS, nor indeed to the statutory services. They raise questions of monitoring and registration which we have not been able to look at. Pending resolution of these wider questions we suggest that Joint Consultative Committees could be appropriate bodies to consider arrangements for the monitoring as well as the planning of services locally, including both statutory and non-statutory provision.

Making progress with limited resources

10.14 We have been ever conscious that the White Paper was over-optimistic in its resource assumptions and that, at least in the short to medium term, the resource position is unlikely to improve significantly.

10.15 It is always important to ensure that available resources are spent wisely; it is even more so when resources are constrained. This is particularly true in the case of capital resources.

10.16 We suggest that any development possible in the next few years should be concentrated in those localities where least provision exists at present. We endorse the priority accorded by many Authorities to supporting mentally handicapped people at home and their families by providing advice and help from staff and from voluntary sources, and by making arrngements for short-term care for assessment, planned treatment and family relief. This should be the first priority in all Areas completely lacking in NHS services at present.

10.17 Any authority contemplating capital investment should hesitate before upgrading existing facilities. Would the money be better spent in making provision off-site for the clients concerned? New NHS facilities should not normally be created in places which are already over-provided. Infilling on existing hospital sites still features in some plans and is virtually never justified. Every health District will need some local NHS services. Where capital resources are available, it would be best to concentrate on providing small units where no facilities exist at present. Both NHS and local authorities are advised to consider the possibility of conversions. Conversion runs less risk of creating new institutions.

10.18 We have seen some suggestions that local authorities should take over responsibility for a number of residential units (and their residents) on large hospital sites. We can see that this might be thought of as an aid to joint planning and as an opportunity for cross-fertilization of ideas. However, we consider that as two sets of authorities would thereby acquire an interest in the site the already substantial difficulties in running down large hospitals would be compounded. Neither do we see what benefit is likely to accrue to the residents. We would therefore advise authorities to consider carefully the consequences of such action.

Planning a new pattern of services
10.19 In Chapter 8 we have drawn attention to the obstacles in the way of moving towards a new pattern of local servies with both the NHS and local authorities playing their part. In chapter 9 we have discussed the important role played by the voluntary and private sectors and how this might be further encouraged.

10.20 There has always been considerable debate about the respective roles of health and local authority services in providing for the needs of mentally handicapped people. The quality of this debate has suffered from an absence of consensus both as to what the needs of mentally handicapped people really are and as to the nature of the help which it is appropriate for particular services to provide, particularly where they overlap, as is the case for many people who require both residential care and some degree of attention from professionals of different kinds. There has also been a lack of alternative types of service to evaluate.

10.21 In fact, any division of responsibility between health and social services, and indeed between those agencies and others such as education and housing authorities and organisations providing sheltered employment, must to some extent be arbitrary. Problems of divided responsibility have led to practical difficulties to which a variety of radical solutions has been suggested. For example, prime responsibility for residential services, domiciliary support and (for adults) training might be laid on either health or social services, with the other providing some services on an agency basis. Another alternative would be to set up a separate mental handicap service. However, the disruption entailed by changes of this magnitude would hae to be weighed against any benefits that might ensue, and substantial changes in responsibility for services are particularly difficult to make at times of constraint or retrenchment.

10.22 We would suggest, therefore, that consideration should be given to less radical changes aimed at reducing the areas of confusion and overlap between the responsibilities of authorities and at improving and encouraging joint working by health, social services and other agencies, including the private and voluntary sectors. This would entail looking at the elements going to make up a service for mentally handicapped people and their families, the extent to which it would be appropriate for each agency to contribute to the provision of these elements, the overall level of service required and mechanisms for joint planning and making the best use of limited financial resources.

The next step

10.23 The disparity between the resource assumptions underlying the White Paper and those which must underlie planning at the present time must obviously cause us to consider whether existing policies need to be adjusted to bring them into line with available resources. Put more bluntly, this means considering whether the policy of building up local services should be abandoned or at least deferred so that whilst the development of local services remained a goal, the existing pattern would remain substntially unchanged until well into the next century.

10.24 We consider, however, that to suggest doing this at the present time would be a counsel of despair. We do see clear evidence that both health and local authorities have, since publication of the White Paper, sought to improve their services for mentally handicapped people, that they have made real increases in expenditure on these services and that notable advances have been made in the direction the White Paper indicated. Community care has expanded, and uneven but real improvements have been made in the facilities and services provided. It is surely right to try and build on this progress rather than abandon it.

10.25 The next step, in our opinion, should therefore be to look at ways of facilitating the change to a pattern of local services. Only if it were to prove impossible to take any action on this front in a reasonable timescale, would we recommend a fundamental change in policy.

Appendix A General Principles

The 1971 White Paper set out the following general principles on which it said current thinking about mental handicap was based.

i   A family with a handicapped member has the same needs for general social services as all other families. The family and the handicapped child or adult also need special additional help, which varies according to the severity of the handicap, whether there are associated physical handicaps or behaviour problems, the age of the handicapped person and his family situation.

ii   Mentally handicapped children and adults should not be segregated unnecessarily from other people of similar age, nor from the general life of the local community.

iii   Full use should be made of available knowledge which can help to prevent mental handicap or to reduce the severity of its effects.

iv   There should be a comprehensive initial assessment and periodic reassessment of the needs of each handicapped person and his family.

v   Each handicapped person needs stimulation, social training and education and purposeful occupation or employment in order to develop to his maximum capacity and to exercise all the skills he acquires, however limited they may be.

vi   Each handicapped person should live with his own family as long as this does not impose an undue burden on them or him, and he and his family should receive full advice and support. If he has to leave home for a foster hom, residential home or hospital, temporarily or permanently, links with his own family should normally be maintained.

vii   The range of services in every area should be such that the family can be sure that their handicapped member will be properly cared for when it becomes necessary for him to leave the family home.

viii   When a handicapped person has to leave his family home, temporarily or permanently, the substitute home should be as homelike as possible, even if it is also a hospital. It should provide sympathetic and constant human relationships.

ix   There should be proper co-ordination in the application of relevant professional skills for the benefit of individual handicapped people and their families, and in the planning and administration of relevant services, whether or not these cross administrative frontiers.

x   Local authority personal social services for the mentally handicapped should develop as an intergral part of the services recently brought together under the Local Authority Social Services Act, 1970.

xi   There should be close collaboration between these services and those provided by other local authority departments (eg child health services and education), and with general practitioners, hospitals and other services for the disabled.

xii Hospital services for the mentally handicapped should be easily accessible to the population they serve. They should be associated with other hospital services, so that a full range of specialist skills is easily available when needed for assessment or treatment.

xiii Hospital and local authority services should be planned and operated in partnership; the Government's proposals for the reorganisation of the National Health Service will encourage the closest co-operation.

xiv Voluntary service can make a contribution to the welfare of mentally handicapped people and their families at all stages of their lives and wherever they are living.

xv Understanding and help from friends and neighbours and from the community at large are needed to help the family to maintain a normal social life and to give the handicapped member as nearly normal a life as his handicap or handicaps permit.

Appendix B Legislation

B.1   The following legislation is of particular relevance to services for mentally handicapped people. The list is not to be considered completely comprehensive — for example, it omits large bodies of legislation, such as that applying to social security and children's legislation, under which mentally handicapped people can benefit in the same way as other citizens.

Disabled Persons (Employment) Act 1944

National Assistance Act 1948 (as amended)

     section 29 (powers and duties of local aurhorities)

  * sections 37–40 (registration of residential homes)

     sections 47 and 48 (removal to suitable premises of persons in need of care and attention and duty of authorities to provide temporary protection for property and persons admitted to hospitals etc).

Sexual Offences Act 1956
     sections 7, 9, 14(4), 15(3), 21, 27, 29, 45 (as amended)

Disabled Persons (Employment) Act 1958

Mental Health Act 1959 (as amended)

     all provisions relating to detention and guardianship
     section 8(2) (applies section 29 of the National Assistance Act 1948 to the mentally disordered)

     section 9 (use of accommodation provided under the Children Acts by mentally disordered children who are not in care)

     section 10 (duty of local authority to arrange visiting of certain hospital patients)

  * sections 19–21 (registration of residential homes)

     section 22 (inspection of premises by mental welfare officers)

     section 128 (unlawful sexual intercourse by hospital staff and guardians with mentally handicapped women under their care)

     section 135 (removal of mentally disordered people needing care and attention)

Sexual Offences Act 1967
   sections 1(3), 1(4)

Chronically Sick and Disabled Persons Act 1970

Education (Handicapped Children) Act 1970

Guardianship Act 1973
   Schedule 1

Nursing Homes Act 1975

National Health Services Act 1977

   sections 1–4 (general duties and powers of the Secretary of State)

   section 13 (power of Secretary of State to give directions)

   section 85 (default powers of Secretary of State in respect of health and local social services authorities)

   Schedule 8, paragraph 2 (powers and duties of local authorities)

Health Services Act 1980

B.2   The following Regulations are relevant:

The National Assistance (Registration of Homes) Regulations 1949 (SI 1949/1622)

The Mental Health Review Tribunal Rules 1960 (SI 1960/1139)

The Mental Health (Powers of Inspection) Regulations 1960 (SI 1960/1160)

The Mental Health (Hospital and Guardianship) Regulations 1960 (SI 1960/1241)

The Mental Health (Registration and Inspection of Mental Nursing Homes) Regulations 1960 (SI 1960/1272)

The National Assistance (Registration of Homes) (Amendment) Regulations 1960 (SI 1960/1273)

The Mental Health (Hospital and Guardianship) Amendment Regulations 1962 (SI 1962/1593)

The Conduct of Mental Nursing Homes Regulations 1962 (SI 1962/1999)

The National Assistance (Conduct of Homes) Regulations 1962 (SI 1962/2000)

The Conduct of Nursing Homes Regulations 1963 (SI 1963/1434)

The Nursing Homes (Registration and Records) Regulations 1974 (SI 1974/22)

The National Health Service Functions (Directions to Authorities) Regulations 1974 (SI 1974/24)

The National Health Service Reorganisation (Consequential Amendments) Order 1974 (SI 1974/241)

The Mental Health (Hospital and Guardianship) Amendment Regulations 1975 (SI 1975/1337)

B.3   Directions have also been given to local authorities in Local Authority Circular 13/74 and Local Authority Circular 19/74, which have effect as if given under paragraph 2 of Schedule 8 to the 1977 (NHS) Act.

---

*These actions are being consolidated by the Residential Homes Bill and will be repealed when the Act comes into force — expected some time in 1980.

Appendix C   Guidance issued by DHSS

Title (and brief summary where required)	No	Date of Issue
C.1 *Short-term care of mental defectives in case of urgency.* Drew attention to the powers under S28 of the NHS Act 1946 whereby local health authorities could provide temporary accommodation for home-based mental defectives in the event of a domestic crisis.	5/52	21 January 1952
C.2 *Bathing of Patients in Mental and Mental Deficiency Hospitals.* Suggested review of arrangements for bathing patients. Local management in consultation with senior nursing staff were asked to ensure that all nursing staff received training on how to ensure safety, hygiene, comfort and privacy of patients during bathing, use of relevant equipment etc.	HM(56)99	27 November 1956
C.3 *Protection of Patients' Property.* Drew attention to fact that patients compulsorily detained in hospital were no longer assumed necessarily incapable of managing their own affairs — the decision would depend on individual capacity.	HM(60)80	5 October 1960
C.4 *Mental Health Act 1959.* Announced the bringing into effect of the remaining provisions of the Mental Health Act 1959 and the Mental Health (Hospital and Guardianship) Regulations 1960 and gave guidance.	HM(60)69	29 August 1969
C.5 *Disposal of Surplus Hospital Land.* Pointed out that unless farming and market gardening activities were necessary to provide training and occupation for patients they should not be continued.	HM(62)46	26 July 1962
C.6 *Improving the Effectiveness of the Hospital Service for the Mentally Subnormal.* De-	HM(65)104	2 December 1965

scribed the functions of the hospital services for the mentally subnormal and stressed the importance of close links with local authority and voluntary services and with the family doctor.

C.7	*Screening for the Early Detection of Phenylketonuria.* Recommended use of the Guthrie Test.	HM(69)72	September 1969
C.8	*Interim Measures to Improve Hospital Services for the Mentally Handicapped.* Advised secretaries to RHBs of a programme of interim improvements (minimum standards).	Letter with RHB Chairmen 10/69	10 December 1969
C.9	*Services for the Mentally Handicapped.* Follow up to item C.8 above.	DS12/71 RHB Chairmen 10/70	5 January 1971
C.10	*Registration of Adult Training Centres under the 1961 Factories Act.* Informed authorities that all ATCs should be so registered.	LASSL 2/71	23 February 1971
C.11	*Better Services for the Mentally Handicapped.* Drew attention to White Paper (Cmnd 4683) which considered how best to provide mentally handicapped people with the full range of services which they need.	LASSL 24/71) LHAL 18/71)	23 June 1971
C.12	*Hospital Memorandum on Patients' Monies.* Consolidated guidance on personal allowances and reward payments to long-stay patients; gave guidance on the issue and use of such money; gave guidance on the custody, investment and disposal of money deposited by patients.	HM(71)90	November 1971
C.13	*Patients Dying in Hospital.* Burial and cremation of patients who die in hospital and related matters.	HM(72)41	July 1972
C.14	*Travelling Expenses and Transport for Hospital Patients and Visits*	HM(73)20	May 1973
C.15	*Employment Medical Advisory Service – Effect on ATCs and Other Centres Registered Under Factories Act 1961.* Drew attention to decision by Department of Employment re S118 of the Act.	LASSL 31/73	7 August 1973

	Title (and brief summary where required)	No	Date of Issue
C.16	*MH Children in Hospitals far from their homes.* Proposed central records for assessing transfers.	DS 212/73	20 August 1973
C.17	*Services for the Mentally Disordered Provided under S12 of the health Services and Public health Act 1968 Replacement of Schemes by Arrangements in consequence of S195 of Local Government Act 1972*	LAC 19/74	23 April 1974
C.18	*Education of Mentally Handicapped Children and Young People in Hospital.* Joint DES/DHSS circular re education of mentally handicapped and other long stay children in hospital — standards of practice and some questions of administration.	Circ 5/74 (DES) HSC(IS)37 (DHSS)	21 May 1974
C.19	*Long Stay Children in Hospital.* Asked Authorities to review provision for long-stay children in the light of this discussion paper and identify what more could be done for them within existing resources.	DS 182/74	26 July 1974
C.20	*Security in NHS Hospitals for The Mentally Ill and Mentally Handicapped.* Gave guidance on services for mentally ill and mentally handicapped patients who although they did not require admission to a Special Hospital, could not satisfactorily be managed in the ordinary wards of psychiatric hospitals.	HSC(IS)61	July 1974
C.21	*Registration of Nursing Homes.* Authorised Area Administrators to refuse or cancel registration of nursing homes under S197 and S188 respectively of the Public Health Act 1936.	HSC(IS)106	January 1975
C.22	*Wheelchair Users in Long-Stay Hospitals.* Recommended that arrangements be made with Manager of the nearest Artificial Limb and Appliance Centre to review wheelchair requirements of permanently disabled children in long-stay hospitals at regular intervals.	HSC(IS)137	April 1975
C.23	*Hospital Farms and Market Gardens.* Asked for a further review of farming activities.	DS 241/75	July 1975
C.24	*Personal Allowances to patients in Mental Hospitals.* New arrangements for payment of personal allowances to certain patients in psychiatric hospitals.	DS 377/75	29 December 1975

	Title (and brief summary where required)	No	Date of Issue
C.25	*The Management of Violent, or Potentially Violent Patients*	HC(76)11	March 1976
C.26	*The Health Advisory Service*	HC(76)21	April 1976
C.27	*Health Building: Cost Allowance for Small Mental Handicap Hospital Units.*	HN(77)58	April 1977
C.28	*Hospital Facilities for Children*	HC(77)30	August 1977
C.29	*Prevention and Health-Reducing the Risk. Safer Pregnancy and Childbirth.* Joint discussion paper by the Health Departments of Great Britain and N. Ireland.	HC(77)36 LAC(77)23	September 1977
C.30	*Court Report on Child Health Services.* Advised authorities of the then Government's conclusions on the recommendations of the Court Committee on Child Health Services (Fit for the Future Cmnd 6684).	HC(78)5 LAC(78)2	January 1978
C.31	*Health Building: Cost Allowances for Health Building, including Residential Accommodation*	HN(78)76	June 1978
C.32	*Development Team for the Mentally Handicapped.* Enclosed copies of the first report of the Development Team.	HN(78)78 LASSL(78)15	June 1978
C.33	*Children in Hospital Maintenance of Family Links.* Stated that children should be admitted to hospital only if there was no satisfactory alternative and should be discharged as soon as possible: when admitted, every attempt should be made to maintain links with the child's parents.	HC(78)28	11 September 1978
C.34	*Helping Mentally Handicapped People in Hospital.* Enclosed an advance copy of the NDG'S 'Helping Mentally Handicapped People in Hospital' and recommended aspects which could be put into practice within existing resources.	HN(78)135 LASSL(78)28	October 1978
C.35	*Psychiatric Hospitals – Notifications to NHS Central Register.* Reminded authorities of the need to continue to notify NHS Central Register of inpatients resident in mental illness or mental handicap hospitals or units for 2 years or longer.	HN(78)148	November 1978

Title (and brief summary where required)	No	Date of Issue
C.36 *Helping Mentally Handicapped People in Hospital.* Enclosed printed copies of report.	HN(78)150 LASSL(78)32	November 1978
C.37 *Report of the Committee of Enquiry into Mental Handicap Nursing and Care.* Informed Health and Local Authorities of publication of the Jay Report and described consultation process.	HN(79)27 LASS(79)6	March 1979
C.38 *Creating a Learning Environment.* Enclosed copies of 'Creating a Learning Environment' a reprint of Chapters 5 and 6 of 'Helping Mentally Handicapped People in Hospital'.	HN(79)55	September 1979
C.39 *Social Security Payments for Hospital In-Patients – November 1979 Uprating.* Notified increases in rates of social security benefits, and included information on extension of mobility allowances, increased pocket money for the mentally handicapped etc.	HN(79)109	November 1979
C.40 *Working Group on Organisational and Management Problems of Mental Illness Hospitals.* Commended to health authorities the report of a Working Group on Organisational and Management Problems of Mental Illness Hospitals and asked for copies to be made available to managers of mental illness and mental handicap hospitals.	HN(80)1	January 1980
C.41 *Adult Training Centres.* Cancels the "Model of Good Practice" on Local Authority Training Centres for Mentally Handicapped Adults issued in 1968 and records the outcome of consultation on suggestions made by the National Development Group for the Mentally Handicapped.	LAC(80)2	19 May 1980
C.42 *Health Service Development: Management and Structure.* Guidance to RHAs and to the new district authorities to implement the changes in structure and management organisation which are needed to fulfil the aims set out in "Patients First".	HC(80)8 LAC(80)3	July 1980
C.43 *The Development of the Community Psychiatric Nursing Service.* Enclosed a discussion paper describing the evolution and present pattern of the community psychiatric nursing service (including community psychiatric nursing services in mental handicap).	CNO(80)7	August 1980

Title	No	Date of Issue
(and brief summary where required)		

C.44   *Design Guidance*

Hospital Building for the Mentally Handicapped. DHSS Design Bulletin 1 (A background to design) DHSS Design Bulletin 2 (A Hospital Unit for Children — Sheffield Type A).

C.45   *Local Authority Building Notes*

1 – Costing and Building Procedures
5 – Adult Training Centres
8 – Residential Accommodation for Mentally Handicapped Adults.

C.46   *Building Guidance.* Includes at Annex III — Health Services Residential Accommodation for the Mentally Handicapped. Interim Building Design Guidance.   HN(80)21   September 1980

Appendix D   The Education of mentally Handicapped Children

Introduction

D.1   This Appendix provides some background information on educational provision made for mentally handicapped children and young people by local education authorities. It gives some statistics of pupil numbers and outlines the policies of the Department of Education and Science and of local education authorities. It covers the past and present positions but does not take into account possible developments following the Warnock Report (see para 2.17).

The Statutory Framework

D.2   Under Section 57 of the Education Act 1944 (as amended by the Mental Health Act 1959) LEAs had a duty to ascertain which children in their area were "suffering from a disability of mind of such a nature or to such an extent as to make them unsuitable for education at school". Such children were generally regarded as ineducable and their treatment, care and training were the responsibility of local health authorities. They attended junior training centres, were in mental handicap hospitals, special care units or private institutions of various kinds or remained at home.

D.3   On 1 April 1971 the Education (Handicapped Children) Act 1970 came into force. Local health authorities lost the power to provide training for mentally handicapped children, and staff and premises were transferred from health authorities to LEAs. Some 400 new special schools were formed from the junior training centres, special care units and hospital provision. Thus, from 1 April 1971, severely mentally handicapped children joined all other children in the education service in England and Wales, and came under the provisions of the Education Acts which apply generally to those requiring special educational treatment.

D.4   The formal categories of pupils requiring special educational treatment (usually now simply called "special education") are laid down in the Handicapped Pupils and Special Schools Regulations 1959. These include a definition of educationally subnormal (ESN) pupils: those "who, by reason of limited ability or other conditions resulting in educational retardation, require some specialised form of education wholly or partly in substitution for the education normally given in ordinary schools". Thus the ESN category includes all children who for any reason show educational attainments significantly below those of their peers and who cannot make progress without special arrangements being made for them. Some of these children can benefit from such arrangements in ordinary schools, whilst others (often those with additional handicaps) require education in a special school or special unit attached to an ordinary school.

D.5   At the time of the transfer of responsibility for mentally handicapped children it was thought inadvisable to designate a new category since to do so might have perpetuated distinctions that the legislation was intended to discontinue. Valid distinctions between children in the existing ESN category and those newly admitted to the education system could not always be made. It was therefore decided to include both groups of children within the educationally subnormal category, but thos does not imply that distinctions between the educational needs of sub-groups within that category are inappropriate and, in practice, two broad groupings have emerged within the educationally subnormal category: moderate — ESN(M), and severe —ESN(S).

D.6   It should be noted that one of the key recommendations in the Warnock Report calls for the abolition of all the statutory categories of handicap in favour of a system for "recording" children who — after multi-professional assessment — are judged by LEAs to require special educational provision not normally available in ordinary schools.

D.7   Local Education Authorities have a duty under Section 34 of the Education Act 1944 to ascertain which children in their areas require special education and to provide it (unless the parents make private arrangements which are acceptable to the authority). The Act lays down procedures for medical examinations of children and the Department of Education and Science has issued comprehensive guidance to LEAs in Circular 2/75 about this and other aspects of discovering, diagnosing and assessing children who require special education. For most mentally handicapped children their disabilities and difficulties will be apparent at an early age and local education authorities will arrange for multi-professional assessments well before the date for starting school: the procedure under Section 34 may be used for a child of two years or over.

Numbers of Children
D.8   About two per cent of all children(*) are at present assessed as handicapped within the meaning of the Handicapped Pupils and Special Schools Regulations 1959: some 168,000 children in England. In Table D.1 below these pupils have been classified according to their major handicap but, of course, the discrete forms of physical or mental disability set out in the Regulations conceal large numbers of children who are multiply-handicapped, and the categories do not indicate the severity of the individual handicaps. All the statistics in this paper exclude ESN pupils placed in ordinary classes in primary and secondary schools, as complete information is not available on

such placements. It is, however, unlikely that any significant numbers of ESN(S) pupils are so placed. The numbers of ESN(M) pupils are therefore understated, perhaps seriously.

*Under the Education Act 1944 "child" means a person who is not over compulsory school age (5–16 years) and therefore includes under-fives, and "pupils" means a person of any age for whom education is required to be provided under the Act. In practice the pupil numbers include 2–19 year olds, the vast majority of whom are aged 5–16 years.

TABLE D.1   Handicapped Pupils[a]

January 1978   England

Main handicap of pupils	Number of pupils	Percentage
ESN(M)	75,679	45.0
ESN(S)	32,362	19.2
Maladjusted	21,079	12.5
Physically Handicapped	15,510	9.2
Other[b]	23,670	14.1
Total	168,300	100.0

[a] The figures in this table are not comparable with those given in table D2 as they are derived from a different source.

[b] Delicate, deaf, partially hearing, blind, partially sighted, epileptic, autistic, speech defective.

Special Schools

D.9   Special schools are those "specially organised for the purpose of providing special educational treatment for pupils requiring such treatment" and approved as such by the Secretary of State for Education and Science. The schools are of two kinds: those maintained by an LEA, and those provided by voluntary bodies (non-maintained special schools). In the case of the latter group of schools fees are charged to the LEA. In Table D.2 the total number of special schools is given, classified by the main handicap for which they cater, together with an analysis of pupil numbers and the numbers of qualified teachers.

TABLE D.2 Special Schools, Pupils and Qualified Teachers[a]

January 1978 England

	Schools			Full-time Pupils				All Qualified Teachers		
	Day	Boarding	In Day Total	In Day Schools	In Boarding Schools Day	Boarding	Total	Full-time	Full-time Equivalent of Part-time	Pupil/Teacher Ratio
Maintained Schools										
ESN(M)	391	106	497	48,592	3,808	5,585	57,985	5,768	149	9.8
ESN(S)*	417	22	439	27,480	1,109	403	28,992	3,629	61	7.9
ESN(M) and (S)	31	7	38	3,891	613	395	4,899	539	8	9.0
All Maintained Schools	1,168	312	1,480	101,055	8,542	13,348	122,945	14,591	427	8.2
Non-Maintained Schools										
ESN(M)	4	11	15	383	49	818	1,250	135	5	8.9
ESN(S)	—	1	1	—	—	49	49	5	—	9.4
All Non-Maintained Schools	10	101	111	921	958	6,701	8,580	1,158	66	7.0
Total	1,178	413	1,591	101,976	9,500	20,049	131,525	15,749	493	8.1

* Including 64 special schools in mental handicap hospital (regarded as day schools).

[a] The figures in this table are not comparable with those given in Tables D1 and D3 as they are derived from a different source.

Types of Provision

D.10 The types of educational provision made for ESN pupils are shown in Table D.3 together with pupil numbers. The statistics have been compiled from returns by local education authorities and record the position in January 1978. It will be seen that the majority of the pupils attend day special schools. Others attend residential special schools, independent schools, designated special classes in primary and secondary schools or receive education outside a school setting, eg in units or groups at various establishments or at home.

TABLE D.3 Educational Provision[a]   January 1978   England

Place of Education	ESN(M)		ESN(S)	
	Number of pupils	Per cent	Number of pupils	Per cent
Maintained special schools				
day pupils	55,087	72.8	24,998	77.2
boarding pupils	6,079	8.0	600	1.9
Non-maintained special schools				
day pupils	390	0.5	17	0.1
boarding pupils	751	1.0	167	0.5
Hospital special schools[b]	51	0.1	3,967	12.3
Designated special classes in primary and secondary schools	8,587	11.3	279	0.9
Independent schools (mainly boarding)	598	0.8	665	2.1
Educated otherwise than at school[c]	335	0.4	792	2.4
Awaiting admission to special schools —				
under 5[d]	167	0.2	509	1.6
5 and over[e]	3,634	4.8	368	1.1
Totals	75,679	100	32,362	100

Notes:

[a] The figures given in this table are not comparable with those given in Table D2 as they are derived from a different source.

[b] Some children in hospitals attend schools in the community and are excluded from this line. At the same time, some hospital schools admit as day pupils children who live in the community.

[c] In units or groups not forming part of a school, or at home with peripatetic teachers.

[d] Some may attend nursery or primary schools whilst awaiting a place in a special school.

[e] Most of these children will be attending primary or secondary schools whilst awaiting a place in a special school.

Education in Hospitals

D.11 There were some 4,000 (12 per cent) ESN(S) pupils on the registers of hospital special schools, mainly in mental handicap hospitals. This number, however, is not equivalent to the number of child patients in mental handicap hospitals because some children in these hospitals attend schools in the community and are counted on the registers of those schools, whilst some hospital special schools admit as day pupils children who live in the community.

D.12   The Department's general policy (in Circular 5/74, "The Education of Mentally Handicapped Children and Young People in Hospital") is that wherever practicable children should go out to a special school serving the community at large. The next best arrangement is for them to go to specially provided educational premises which form a special school within the confines of the hospital. Where educational premises do not exist or are inadequate the children should be taught in suitable hospital accommodation normally used for other purposes or, very exceptionally, in the wards themselves. In the latter cases, the circular underlines the importance of preserving the idea that children "go to school" and are not interrupted by ward routines while schooling is in progress.

Appendix E Employment Opportunities for Mentally Handicapped People

The Careers Service

E.1   The Careers Service is maintained by local education authorities under the guidance in England of the Secretary of State for Employment. The great majority of young people aged 16 and 17 choose to use the careers service rather than MSC's Employment Service which is also available to them. The Careers Service is thus used by many handicapped young people. Reluctance to register as disabled is even more marked amongst young people, particularly those who are mentally handicapped, than it is among adults. Of all the disabled young people (both registered and unregistered) seen by Careers Officers, just under half are mentally handicapped.

E.2   The Manpower Services Commission (MSC) has responsibility for policy on and operation of all the main services concerned with the employment, rehabilitation and training of disabled people. The MSC also services the National Advisory Council on Employment of Disabled People.

The Disablement Resettlement

E.3   Mentally handicapped people, like all disabled people, may avail themselves of the services of the MSC's Disablement Resettlement Officers (there are over 500 DROs in the country involved in placement work). DROs help disabled people to choose, train for, obtain and keep worthwhile jobs, and the MSC has various grants available to assist in this — such as assistance with fares to work, or finance to adapt employers' premises.

Employment Rehabilitation

E.4   The MSC operates a national network of 27 Employment Rehabilitation Centres (ERCs) which provide employment rehabilitation and assessment services for people experiencing difficulty in entering or re-joining the employment field following illness, injury or long term unemployment. 428 mentally handicapped people attended ERCs in 1977, representing 3.1% of the total ERC throughput. A feature of 17 ERCs at present is Young Persons Work Preparation Courses for young people over 16 years old who are unlikely to find or obtain permanent employment without some form of work preparation or assessment. The courses combine remedial education facilities provided by local education authorities with the work preparation and assessment facilities of the ERCs, and usually last 12 weeks. As a general pattern, 60% of entrants are Educationally Sub-Normal (Moderate) from special schools. About 35% have physical or perceptual problems. 789 young people completed a course during the year ending March 1979. These courses received favourable mention in the Warnock Committee's Report, and it is now planned to extend them to all ERCs wherever possible as part of MSC's contribution to the Youth Opportunity Programme.

Sheltered Employment

E.5   Under the MSC's scheme of grants, sheltered workshops and Remploy factories provide employment for over 13,000 severely disabled people. Over 10% of the 8,000 people in Remploy factories are mentally handicapped. In addition, employment for the mentally handicapped is provided in sheltered workshops and sheltered industrial groups.

Training

E.6   MSC's Training Services Division has a basic policy objective of meeting the training needs, wherever possible, of disabled people who are suitable for vocational training for open employment. This does not include severely mentally handicapped people, but those at the higher end of the ability range of mild mental handicap can, and do, take advantage of the following facilities: Work Introduction Courses, Short Training Courses, Individual Training throughout with an Employer and other Training Opportunities Scheme courses. In addition, Queen Elizabeth's Residential College at Leatherhead runs two industrial training and work experience courses for people with low ability, and some of the trainees are mentally handicapped.

Experimental/Innovatory Services

E.7   In April 1978, MSC's Special Programmes Division launched their new schemes. The Special Temporary Employment Programme aims to help unemployed adults improve their prospects of obtaining jobs by providing short-term worthwhile employment, and although no special provision is made for the mentally handicapped, many do participate in these schemes. The Youth Opportunity Programme for those aged 16 to 18 provides work preparation and work experience. Some discretion is allowed in applying the rules governing both entry and length of stay. This discretion is applied for certain disadvantaged young people including those who are mentally handicapped. Additionally, the MSC, aware that handicapped people in general may be missing out on their fair share of opportunities, set up a working group to look at their involvement in Special Programmes. As a result of the work done by this group, it is intended to publish a document, which it is hoped will stimulate interest in handicapped people's problems and advise on how opportunities can be developed within special programmes.

Appendix F   Definitions of mental Handicap

Definitions of Mental Handicap

White Paper "Better Services for the Mentally Handicapped"
"A person who is mentally handicapped does not develop in childhood as quickly as other children nor attain the full mental capacities of a normal adult".

Mental Health Act 1959
....." "severe subnormality" [mental handicap] means a state of arrested or incomplete development of mind which includes subnormality of intelligence and is of such a nature or degree that the patient is incapable of living an independent life or of guarding himself against serious exploitation, or will be so incapable when of an age to do so".

White Paper "Review of the Mental Health Act 1959"
"A state of arrested or incomplete development of mind which includes significant impairment of intelligence and social functioning". The definition of severe mental handicap includes severe impairment of intelligence and social functioning.

American Association on Mental Deficiency:
"Significantly sub-average general intellectual functioning existing concurrently with deficits in adaptive behaviour and manifested during the developmental period".

International Classification of Diseases:
"A condition of arrested or incomplete development of mind which is especially characterised by subnormality of intelligence. The assessment of intellectual level should be based on whatever information is available including clinical evidence, adaptive behaviour and psychometric findings".

Appendix G Case Registers and Client Characteristics

G.1   The following Case Registers for the Mentally Handicapped in England, mentioned in Chapter 3, helped us with our work on prevalence and use of services for the mentally handicapped:

Camberwell Case Register   (set up 1967)
Population covered 140,000 approx
Average prevalence rate 3.3/1000 population

Lambeth Case Register   (set up 1977)
Population covered 270,000 approx
Average prevalence rate 3.4/1000 population

Salford Case Register   (set up 1961)
Population covered 250,000 approx
Average prevalence rate 3.4/1000 population

Sheffield Case Register   (Set up 1975)
Population covered 550,000 approx
Average prevalence rate 2.9/1000 population

Wessex Case Register   (set up 1963)
Population covered 2,700,000 approx
Average prevalence rate 2.9/1000 population

G.2   The uses of Case Registers fall into three main categories:

a   as a data bank for research:

b   as an information system for service planning, and monitoring:

c   as a means of co-ordinating information about individual clients and the services being provided for them.

G.3   The existing registers in England were established in various ways and for differing purposes. Those in Camberwell and Salford were primarily intended as bases for research, although both have now been modified to serve other purposes; the Camberwell Register is funded by the Medical

Research Council, whilst Salford which was originally wholly funded by DHSS is now supported largely by the AHA: the Wessex Register was intended for service planning and as a data bank for individual clients' histories, and it is financed by the RHA; the Sheffield Register was started using DHSS funds as an experiment in providing and maintaining an integrated, comprehensive information service for the mentally handicapped. It is now financed by the AHA. The Lambeth register has principally a service planning function and was set up and financed by the Local Authority, in conjunction with the AHA.

Appendix H Powers for the provision of transport

H.1   Health authorities may provide transport services for those for whom they are responsible under Section 3 of the NHS Act 1977; social services departments may do so under the National Assistance Act; up to the age of 16 local education authorities may provide transport between a child's home (including a hospital or a hostel within this definition) and his school. Where a school is provided in large hospital grounds however, advice has been given (Joint Circular 5/76 (DES)/HSC(IS)37(DHSS)) that health authorities should provide the necessary transport. Disputes have arisen over transport from hospital to ATCs. Whilst it is for local decision which authority should provide transport, it usually falls to the AHA to provide transport for people living in hospitals.

H.2   Shortages in ambulance provision may mean that day hospital places cannot be taken up. In providing facilities therefore, authorities need to consider carefully the type of transport required and who should provide it. JCPTs can provide an important service in considering this issue.

H.3   Exemption from Public Service vehicle licensing regulations and relaxation of the bus licensing laws by virtue of the Transport Act 1978 now make it easier for voluntary organisations to establish community bus services in both urban and rural areas. Circular HC(78)44 recommended to health authorities that they should consider giving assistance to organisations seeking to establish such a service where it would benefit the NHS. This could be done by giving estimates of the demands patients, staff and visitors might make on such a service if it included a hospital on its route, lending vehicles to organisations when their own is out of use, providing NHS accommodation for garaging, or contributing to the setting up of the service. Such measures could help isolated hospitals where it has been difficult to maintain links between patients and their families, or to obtain staff. Community buses could also be hired for social outings when not required for their regular journeys. Social car schemes — car sharing for payment towards expenses — were also made possible under the Transport Act 1978 and health authorities may promote such schemes in co-operation with voluntary bodies, for use of staff, out-patients or visitors.

H.4   A number of mentally handicapped people will, like everyone else, use normal public transport facilities in order to travel to work or home for the weekend from the hospital or hostel where they live. Hospital authorities may provide money for their expenses and an escort if it is considered medically necessary. Local authorities have powers under Section 29 of the National Assistance Act to arrange concessionary bus travel for mentally handicapped people in their area, although not all authorities exercise this option.

Printed in the UK for HMSO by Delco Printing Co.Ltd.
Dd 240258 C8 2/87